RESIST!

A grassroots collection
of stories, poetry, photos and analysis
from the FTAA protests in Québec City and beyond

Words and images of activists, writers, artists,
filmmakers, journalists, students and workers
from across Canada and the United States

Compiled by
Jen Chang, Bethany Or, Eloginy Tharmendran, Emmie Tsumura,
Steve Daniels and Darryl Leroux

Fernwood Publishing • Halifax

Editing: Donna Davis
Drawings: Emmie Tsumura
Cover photo: Jo-Anne McArthur
Design: Brenda Conroy and Beverley Rach
Printed and bound in Canada by: Hignell Printing Limited

A publication of:
Fernwood Publishing
Box 9409, Station A
Halifax, Nova Scotia
B3K 5S3

Fernwood Publishing Company Limited gratefully acknowledges the financial support of the Department of Canadian Heritage, the Nova Scotia Department of Tourism and Culture and the Canada Council for the Arts for our publishing program.

NOVA SCOTIA
Tourism and Culture

Le Conseil des Arts   The Canada Council
du Canada   for the Arts

National Library of Canada Cataloguing in Publication Data

Main entry under title:

Resist!: a grassroots collection of stories, poetry, photos and analysis from the FTAA protests in Québec City and beyond: words and images of activists, writers, artists, filmmakers, journalists, students and workers from across Canada and the United States

Includes bibliographical references.
ISBN 1-55266-063-X

1. Protest movements—Quebec (Province) 2. Social justice—Quebec (Province) 3. Free Trade Area of the Americas (Organization) I. Chang, Jen

JC328.3.R48 2001   322.4'09714   C2001-901586-0

Contents

Acknowledgements

First and foremost, we would like to thank all those who submitted, advised, publicized and encouraged us in the book-making process. Every single correspondence, whether by e-mail, in person or by telephone, was an appreciated and essential part of the process. Without these contacts, we would never have been able to include such a diversity of voices in this book—each one of you is important (including you who are reading this book!). Thank you!

Thanks should also go to our family and friends, who supported and encouraged us along the way. In particular, conversations with Raphaël Thierrin, Isabel Macdonald and Sarah Lamble have helped to shape the content and structure of this book. Special thanks to Nicole, Richard, Shawn and Namitha and her family, who welcomed our "office" into their home.

A big thank-you is also due the wonderful team at Fernwood, especially Bev and Errol, whose support and guidance have made this project a reality.

We thank the Straight Goods team, *rabble.ca,* the folks at the FTAA diary website and, of course, Indymedia, all of whom have contributed greatly to this project.

Finally, we would like to thank each other! This project has been a rewarding group experience during which each of us has learned and grown greatly.

Contributors

T.M. Abdelazim is a writer who moves between Saranac Lake and San Francisco. He is currently working on a collection of short stories, *Things Slip In and Out*, and a collection of political essays, many of which can be found at his website: *www.modocpress.homestead.com*.

Sandra Alland is a queer feminist writer, performer, photographer and activist. She thinks capitalism sucks.

Anon Ymous is Thamil.

Blair Anundson is currently attending Allegheny College in Meadville, Pennsylvania. He enjoys his bass guitar, punk and running around naked.

Jennifer Bennett is Ojibwe/Odawa and a registered member of the Wikwemikong Band on Manitoulin Island, Ontario. A recent graduate of Cornell University, she is currently working towards her licence to become a professional engineer in Ontario and is employed at a Native-owned civil engineering firm building municipal works for First Nations in Ontario.

Angela Bischoff is an activist, writer and environmentalist currently living in Toronto.

Brian Burch is a Toronto-based activist, direct-action trainer and freelance writer. He lives in, is employed by and devotes his free time to the co-op housing movement.

Laura Burrows (a.k.a. Blaze) is a student activist involved in various community actions within the anti-globalization/capitalist movement. She is the co-organizer of "Communal Hearts," a weekly volunteer food donation team for Oshawa kitchens and shelters.

Jen Chang is a Korean-Canadian feminist and a member of the editorial collective. She lives wherever the sun shines and the birds sing, although there seems to be less of each in Toronto these days.

Steve Daniels is a photographer, filmmaker and member of the editorial collective.

Sujata Dey is a community activist, freelance journalist and book publicist living in Montréal. She has been involved in social justice and community radio since 1993. She lost her wallet and mind in Québec City and looks forward to receiving any information on the whereabouts of either.

Erin George is a journalism student who never subscribed to the false notion of objectivity. She has reported on and photographed a number of demonstrations including the recent manifestations in Québec City. When not covering events she is building them. While completing her bachelor of journalism degree, George was a student union leader at Ryerson Polytechnic University and Ontario Chairperson of the Canadian Federation of Students. Her next assignment is Genoa, Italy, for the demonstrations against the G8.

Anup Grewal is a graduate student at Trent University. She is researching Chinese women's writing in the Mao and post-Mao eras of the People's Republic.

Philippe de Grosbois is a 23-year-old francophone student of sociology at the University of Québec in Montréal and is also an active member of the Anti-Capitalist Convergence (CLAC). He is mostly preoccupied with the corporatization of life by individualism and by the impacts of mass culture on our lives.

Scott Harris is an executive producer of *Between The Lines* a nationally syndicated weekly radio newsmagazine in the U.S., originating from WPKN Radio in Bridgeport, Conn.

Caitlin Hewitt-White is a white feminist activist who currently lives and writes in Guelph, Ontario. Her essay is based on research done for her undergraduate thesis at the University of Waterloo. She is active in the Guelph Action Network and the Peak Collective.

Pauline Hwang is a writer and community organizer living in Montréal.

Ali Kazimi's films, *Narmada: A Valley Rises* (1994), *Shooting Indians* (1997) and *Some Kind of Arrangement* (1997), have won over fifteen awards and honours both nationally and internationally. Born and raised in India, he came to Toronto in 1983 and became a Canadian citizen in 1993. He is on the national and Toronto-chapter boards of the Canadian Independent Film Caucus.

Stephan Kim is a student activist in Toronto. He is around 5´10˝ and has dark brown eyes. He is in great physical shape and on weekends likes to go rock climbing, kayaking, parasailing and skydiving. He has an instructor's certificate in deep-ocean scuba diving and in his spare time writes romantic poetry.

Sarah Lamble dreams of one day being a "professional protester" so that she can join the ranks of all the hardcore hooligans whom no one has ever seen but about whom everyone has heard. In the meantime, Sarah spends her days stirring up trouble at Trent University, hanging out at the Ontario Public Interest Research Group in Peterborough and plotting to overthrow the corporate elite of the planet.

Darryl Leroux is a writer and member of the editorial collective. He likes people way more than he likes capital and has been caught talking to himself.

Liberty is a 19-year-old student from Southern California.

Heather Majaury is Myrriah Xochitl Gomez-Majaury's mother. She is an activist, actor, director and playwright. In her current working life she is a journalist and is the Spoken Word Coordinator at CJAM 91.5 FM in Windsor, Ontario. She is also working on a one-woman stage play entitled "Walk Me Around the Medicine Wheel," which she hopes to stage in the early fall.

Anna Manzo is the web editor/producer of "Between the Lines," a syndicated weekly radio newsmagazine. She has also written for *Toward Freedom, Dollars and Sense, E: The Environmental Magazine, the Progressive Media Project, Fairfield County Magazine* and others.

Tullia Marcolongo's most recent work focuses on environmental justice in relation to land-use planning in Ontario. She helps to raise awareness and mobilize her community on the FTAA and corporate control.

Jo-Anne McArthur is a freelance documentary photographer currently living in Toronto.

Leslie Menagh is food issues activist. She is a local organizer and promoter of community shared agriculture.

Emma Mirabella-Davis is a filmmaker, activist and underground cartoonist. Ze lives in New York City and organizes Elkcreek Cinema, a rag-tag tribe of backwoods, anti-corporate artists. The forests of upstate are hir natural habitat.

Kagiso Molope is a South African woman who immigrated to North America in 1997. She works with refugees and homeless people, and in 1998 she made a documentary film about the effects of apartheid on the mental health of Black South African women. She lives and writes in Ontario.

Gian Mura got arrested for the first time after stopping a bulldozer during the building the Cheekeye–Dunsmuir line in the mid-'90s. In the '90s he also started doing anti-poverty activism. He has been a member of OCAP for the past three years and writes poetry and songs in both English and Italian. When he has time and money, he paints and makes statues.

Norman Nawrocki is a Montréal-based author, actor, musician and anarchist. His last book was *No Masters! No Gods! Dare to Dream.* His last CD, *Jesus was Gay*, was with his band, Rhythm Activism. (See more at *www.nothingness.org/music/rhythm.*)

Bethany Or is a member of the editorial collective. She is an artist currently living in Ottawa, Ontario.

Vincent Pang is an amateur photographer, photographs are his visual diary.

François Pelletier is a freelance journalist living in Québec City. His essay first appeared on the Québec City Indymedia site.

Ladner Reet is a poet and artist. She is from beautiful Prince Edward Island.

Alexis Robie is an independent documentarian living in Gowanus, Brooklyn. His next film will be an exploration of the history and politics of borders. He dreams of free and fair media which all people can take part in creating. (More information at *www.tinymedia.com.*)

Malcolm Rogge is a writer, poet and multimedia artist based in Toronto. He has written for *BUST* magazine, *Fuzzy Heads Are Better,* the *Texas International Law Journal*, *Valparaiso's Journal of Third World Legal Studies* and a few other unlikely publications. He is a member of the Toronto Video Activist Collective and the Liaison of Independent Filmmakers of Toronto.

Jeff Shantz is a member of the OCAP executive and works out of the Parkdale office in Toronto. He is co-host of OCAP radio on community stations CHRY 105.5 FM (Thursday 12–1pm) and CKLN 88.1 FM (Friday 6:20–6:40pm). Since Québec City, he has been busy organizing in Windsor for the OCAP-initiated fall actions.

Max Spencer and Nox – The latter is an admirer of anarchist, surreal and contestatory theories and an enthusiast admirer of emperor penguins and snow geese. His contribution to this analysis highlights his subversive and revolutionary ideas. The former is a refined fan of good wine and alternate raptures. His rebellious spirit and gang rhetoric make him the precious element (?) of a public relations agency that he infiltrated a couple of years ago. The combination of their experiences laid down the basis of this analysis.

Darren Stewart grew up in Victoria, British Columbia, and has worked for various media—independent, corporate and otherwise. He recently started a webzine with friends at *www.forgetmagazine.com*. He is currently working for the *Edmonton Journal* and missing the west coast.

Eloginy Tharmendran loves the ocean, warm places and movement. Her most influential teachers have been young humans and various non-human friends, from whom she continues to learn. She is also a member of the editorial collective.

Emmie Tsumura is a Japanese-Canadian artist from Oshawa, Ontario, and a member of the editorial collective. She would like to apologize in advance for staring inappropriately. She loves and hates most people.

Scott Weinstein organized for the FTAA Québec protests by helping with the Creative Action Trainings for street activists and the Québec Medical 2001 team. Rather than "summit-hopping," he remains part of a loose pack of activists stalking the wild capitalists. While not achieving his goal of sleeping in the middle of the Québec protests, he did manage to sleep well at night, knowing that the protests were in good hands.

Anne Marie Wierzbicki is a labour educator currently working in community and labour arts development. She loves to write, work on collaborative arts projects and tend to her tiny garden in Toronto.

Greg Younger-Lewis went to Québec City as an independent journalist from Ottawa and currently works as a reporter at *The Standard* in St. Catharines.

List of Acronyms

Untangling the alphabet soup...

CASA: Summit of the Americas Welcoming Committee (French acronym)
CD: civil disobedience
CIA: Central Intelligence Agency
CLAC: Anti-Capitalist Convergence (French acronym)
CMAQ: Centre for Media Alternatives of Québec (Indymedia Québec)
CSIS: Canadian Security Intelligence Service
EU: European Union
FBI: Federal Bureau of Investigation
FTAA: Free Trade Area of the Americas
G-20: Group of Twenty countries
GMO: genetically modified organisms
GOMM: Group Against the Globalization of Markets (French acronym)
IMC: Independent Media Centre, or Indymedia
IMF: International Monetary Fund
NATO: North Atlantic Treaty Organization
NAFTA: North American Free Trade Agreement
NCCRA: National Community and Campus Radio Association
NDP: New Democratic Party
NGO: non-governmental organization
OAS: Organization of American States
OCAP: Ontario Coalition Against Poverty
OQP2001: Opération Québec Printemps 2001
RCMP: Royal Canadian Mounted Police
WB: World Bank
WTO: World Trade Organization
ZLEA: Zone de libre échange des Amériques (French acronym for FTAA)

March, looking down the hill from Sainte-Claire. (Photo: Vincent Pang)

Note from the Editorial Collective

We would like to clarify a number of the terms that will appear in this book. First, the three colour-coded "zones" or actions frequently referred to—green, yellow and red—existed not necessarily as fixed geographical areas but as flexible spaces in which certain types of actions were to take place. Areas were colour-coded according to the risk of arrest associated with the actions in question. The green zone involved actions for which there was no or a low risk of arrest, and it was more festival-like in nature. The yellow zone involved a moderate risk of arrest for acts of civil disobedience, and it functioned as a possible source of support for those in red actions. The red zone was characterized by actions for which there was a high risk of arrest, and it respected a diversity of tactics, including direct action. Of course, as became obvious throughout the unfolding events, these zones were designed more in theory than in practice. The colour zones were created before the actions in Québec by organizers who perceived a need to accommodate certain groups and individuals, to facilitate a respect for a diversity of tactics among protesters, and to distinguish between the state-sanctioned legal and the illegal forms of protest. As many can attest, the security forces did not respect the idea behind the different zones. Most zones became red. The various police forces arbitrarily tear gassed, shot, beat and arrested people in all three zones, at any given time.

Second, contributors to this book use divergent terminology to describe the security perimeter: the perimeter, the perimeter zone, the unsecured perimeter area, the security zone, the secure area, the fence and the Wall of Shame. All terms refer to the same physical barrier and the consequent security area created by the three-metre-high, nearly four-kilometre-long security fence erected around the downtown core of Québec City. Throughout most of the week, police forces remained behind the physical barrier, venturing out of the secure area only to intensify their attacks with tear gas and rubber and plastic bullets and to make arrests.

Map 1

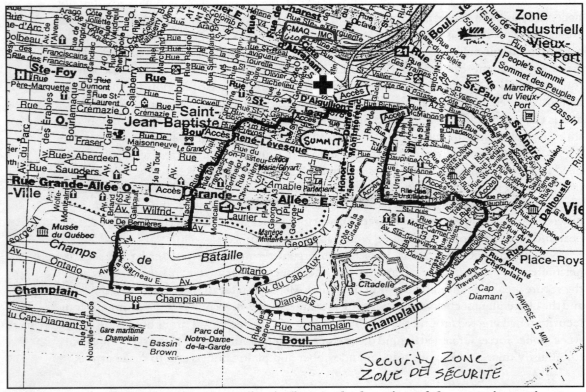

Activist's map of Quebec City. Heavy line indicates the location of the security perimeter. The cliff face was used as a natural barrier (dashed line). CMAQ is the alternative media center head quarters. + = medical center. (Raphaël Thierrin and Steve Daniels)

Map 2

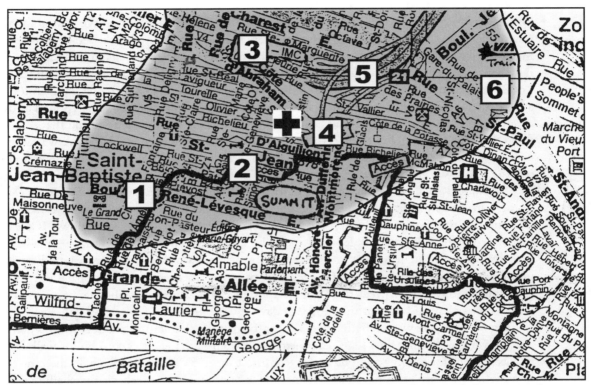

Detail of Quebec City indicating the security perimeter (heavy line) and the approximate area of tear gas deployment (thin line, grey area). 1) The site of the CLAC/CASA action on Friday April 20th. It was at this intersection that the wall first came down. 2) Site of many of the Rue St. Jean actions. Designated as a green-zone on Friday, it became red when the fence was breached on Saturday. 3) Alternative media center. 4) Site of the GOMM action on Friday and continued confrontation during the days that followed. 5) l'Ilôt Fleuri, end point of the candle-light march from Laval, beginning of Thursday night's celebration, home of both the free kitchen and green zone actions. 6) Gathering area and starting point for Saturday's March. + = medical center. The medical center, sites 3 and 5 were all directly tear gassed by police, despite their green zone designations and distance from the perimeter. (Raphaël Thierrin and Steve Daniels)

Publisher's Foreword

On Friday, April 20, my family—me, my partner Beverley and our children Jesse, age 11, and Myah, age 7—arrived in Québec City by car. We had left Halifax a day earlier and drove unimpeded into the city via Boulevard Laurier. There was only light traffic. We waited for a few traffic lights. Nothing suggested that we were driving into a city blockaded by a three-metre-high steel link fence, but we knew it was there because it had been talked about in every newspaper and on every airwave broadcast. We proceeded north along Laurier to Chemin St-Louis and Grande Allée, where we saw a police blockade. We made a U-turn on Grande Allée, a right turn onto Avenue Cartier, proceeded west on Cartier for a city block, then pulled into an empty parking space and got out of our car. On checking the meter we found that there was a two-hour parking limit. Expecting to have to walk a number of blocks before we came even close to where something might be happening, we decided not to feed the meter and pay the fine if we got a ticket.

We walked a half block west on Cartier towards Boulevard René-Lévesque. Suddenly we found ourselves surrounded by a large number of young people, many with teary eyes, some washing out their eyes with water. They had been tear gassed a block or so down René-Lévesque where the chain link fence blocked the street. I was not surprised that people had been tear gassed; I had heard that the police were using gas. I was surprised that we could drive unimpeded to within two blocks of the fence, park our car in a vacant parking space and step right into the fray. It was surreal. For me that experience was a foreshadowing of much of what I saw and participated in over the next two days.

On Saturday we were able to drive our car to a parking lot across the street from where people were assembling for a mass demonstration march—no need to take a bus or walk for blocks. Except for the lingering odour of tear gas, it seemed like a normal day in the city—no visible police presence, no squad cars, no police on foot or on horseback, marshalling the crowd. All of the police were up behind the fence, protecting the free trade negotiators. It seemed like the rest of the city had been given over to the people.

The starting time for the march had been announced for noon but it didn't get started until after 1pm. My family and I waited with friends as thousands upon thousands of people massed, preparing to march south on Charest. The march began. We were close to the head of the crowd, and as we walked towards the intersection of Charest and Couronne we encountered two groups of people. One group urged the marchers to turn right on Couronne; the other urged us to turn left. I heard one voice yell out, "People left, trade unions right." "What is this all about?" I thought. We turned left, in the direction that the pompom-waving cheerleaders were pointing. As it turned out, right took people away from the barricade to a large park five or six kilometres to the west. Left took us towards the hill where the chain link fence was mounted and where a number of people had gone to confront the barricade.

As we approached, the smell of tear gas became increasingly uncomfortable. I hesitated about going closer because of the children, but my son Jesse wanted to go further up the hill. Expecting to be able to stop before the gas got too bad, we continued on. People coming down the hill warned us that the tear gas was bad, and I could see smoke trails as the police launched canister after canister of tear gas into the crowd. Suddenly the gas hit. I could not see. I did not know where I was. I held on to the leash that attached me to Jesse as if it were a lifeline. I did not want him to disappear. As I fumbled to get a water bottle out of my backpack, a medic told me to kneel down and she washed my eyes out with water. Soon I could see again and Jesse was okay. We walked back down the hill, and for the rest of the afternoon we mingled with people on the street and watched from a café as people marched by. I saw many who had followed the crowd to the right, coming back and going up towards the barricade. Some I knew. Some told me that they felt they had been led astray. Later that evening some friends who had been up at the fence told me about what went on, how the fence had been toppled, how people had been targeted and hit with tear-gas canisters, how teddy bears had been catapulted over the fence. Later in the evening, I was told, people who were in a park—some singing, some talking and some dancing—were attacked by police with tear gas. Over two hundred were arrested. One group told of being tear gassed in the back of a locked police van. The police chose the cover of darkness, where they were hidden from the eye of the camera, to launch a terrorist attack.

When talking about the police we need to be reminded that they were acting under the tacit approval, if not the order, of Jean Chrétien and the Liberal government. The prime minister and the government authorities responsible for summit security went out of their way to create the impression that there were "peaceful" and "violent" protesters. This jibed with the concept of democracy that they wanted to portray. They wanted people to believe that only "peaceful" protest is okay in a "democratic" society. They also wanted to popularize the notion that the police were restrained in the face of "violence." They were intent on convincing everyone possible that protesters who challenged the police and the fence, which fortified the hemispheric leaders, were irresponsible and violent. As long as protesters marched away from the barricades, they were lauded. After all, you must be able to expect free speech in a democracy. What is important for the FTAA architects, the prime minister and the hemispheric leaders is that "free" speech does not interfere with the proceedings or the outcome of the negotiations. We should not forget that it was the prime minister, the heads of government and their corporate masters who perpetrated the violence through the actions of the police.

When we first arrived a white police van pulled up and seven or eight black-clothed police officers, some with gas masks, jumped out only feet away from my seven-year-old daughter Myah, who asked, "Who are those men, daddy?" When I told her they were police, she said, "But the police are supposed to help people." It is painful to destroy the illusions of a young child, and it is hard to explain to her that, at least in this case, the police were there to help the people who were negotiating the FTAA agreement on behalf of corporate interests.

It was also painful to see other political and trade union leaders join with Chrétien to perpetuate the idea of "peaceful" and "violent" protesters. Alexa McDonough, the leader of the New Democratic Party, called the people who turned to the left towards the barricade "hoodlums."

The number of marchers was estimated at forty to sixty thousand. Had there been a million, they still would have had little impact on the hemispheric negotiators if they had been led many kilometres away from where the negotiations were taking place. I am not suggesting that all of those people should have gone into the tear-gas zone, but had they all massed on the hill in close proximity to the barricade, their impact would have been far greater. Marching in the opposite direction, as they did, helped Chrétien sell his idea of democracy while negotiating away our freedom.

Finally I want to laud the actions of the young people that I saw. I have been at many such protests in the past forty years, yet I have never before witnessed the discipline and order that prevailed among the people who marched towards the barricades. People were talking to people, helping people and encouraging people. There was a large contingent of medics helping those who were in trouble, suffering from the burning of tear gas, the impact of thrown tear-gas canisters and the injuries caused by rubber and plastic bullets. In the pages of this book you will read their stories. You will see the pictures of their actions, and you will become aware that today's youth are not standing by while their so-called "democratic" political leaders attempt to negotiate away their future in the service of global capitalism. I came away from Québec with renewed vigour, renewed energy and a renewed determination to do all I can to ensure that these young people have a chance to live in a free society with the right to participate in determining their future. I am honoured that Fernwood Publishing has been asked to publish this book.

Errol Sharpe
Publisher

Marchers move towards the perimeter. (Photo: Emmie Tsumura)

Introduction

Background

In April 20–22, 2001, the Summit of the Americas was held in Québec City, the picturesque capital of the province of Québec and a UNESCO World Heritage Site. It was the third such summit. At the first summit, which was held in Miami in 1994 and organized by the Organization of American States (OAS), negotiations for the Free Trade Area of the Americas (FTAA) agreement were initiated. At that meeting, thirty-four heads of state from North, Central and South America and the Caribbean committed to creating the FTAA agreement and completing it by 2005. At the second summit in Santiago in April 1998, a Trade Negotiations Committee (TNC) was set up. It created nine negotiating groups, which have since been meeting frequently.

This year thirty-four heads of state attended the summit in Québec, where one of the main foci was the eventual implementation of the FTAA agreement, the largest trade agreement in the world. The FTAA promises to extend the North American Free Trade Agreement (NAFTA) to the entire Western hemisphere, further widening inequality between and within countries.

In response to the clandestine negotiating process of the FTAA and its potential harmful effects on the environment, human rights, health, education and labour, thousands of people, so-called "protesters," converged on the city to voice their opposition to "free market" logic, corporate-driven globalization and capitalism.

In preparation for the gathering, Canadian authorities organized the largest police deployment in Canadian history—a force that included four levels of police and the Canadian Armed Forces. Nearly ten thousand officers and personnel were deployed throughout the summit and a three-metre-high, 3.8-kilometre-long concrete and chain link fence was built around the downtown core of the city to "protect" the delegates. The cost of security operations alone exceeded Cdn$100 million.

Quite predictably, the security measures resulted in many clashes between police and protesters at or near the fence. From Friday, April 20, to Sunday, April 22, the various police forces unleashed 5192 tear gas canisters on people in the streets, residents of the city and, to some extent, delegates themselves. Along with that, they fired 903 rubber or plastic bullets into crowds or directly at individuals, often at close range.

The Project

This project began as a discussion between friends about the FTAA and the importance of documenting events in Québec and throughout the hemisphere—minus the corporate media lens. Since the protests in Québec, however, the project has changed from a purely documentary effort to include more reflection and analysis of the so-called "anti-globalization" movement and its true revolutionary potential. Through it all, we believe more than ever before that we must keep working, mobilizing, raising awareness and resisting in our local communities if there is to be any hope of sustaining and developing movements against the globalizers' neo-liberal agenda.

Despite our efforts, this is by no means an all-inclusive contribution to the struggle. Many barriers to participation existed throughout the production process. Most notably, since much of the work was done in a very short time frame through e-mail and the internet (as most of the "anti-globalization" movement's efforts seem to have been), our contact with those who don't have access to such media of communication has been drastically limited. Another barrier to participation was geography. Since we all lived in Ontario at the onset of the project, most of our outreaching efforts were directed to individuals, communities and organizations in this area, making many of our contributors Ontarians.

Aside from these and other barriers, we believe this book provides a space for discussion and reflection that will move communities of resistance forward. In it, various opinions are expressed and stories are shared, representing a myriad of experiences and viewpoints. We hope you enjoy what follows.

Banner in front of a residence near the wall of shame. (Photo: Tricia Bell)

declaring freedom

The Struggle for Water: The Cochabamba Declaration

The Editorial Collective

The Cochabamba Declaration was drawn up in reaction to Bechtel Enterprises' privatization of the water system and the subsequent drastic increase in the price of water in the city of Cochabamba, Bolivia.

In January 2000, the government of Bolivia signed a forty-year lease with Bechtel, a San Franciso-based multinational corporation, giving them control of the country's water supply. Bechtel's newly formed subsidary, Aguas del Tunari, was guaranteed a 16 percent average annual return on its investment. In January, residents saw the price of water jump 100 percent or more. Many people could no longer afford water, as water bills reached Cdn$20 or more per month in a country where minimum wage is less that Cdn$60 per month.

This negotiation was part of the World Bank's decades-long push on Majority World countries, including Bolivia, towards the privatization of publicly owned industries by large foreign investors. The Bolivian government has already sold of many of its public institutions, including its airline, several electric utilities and its national railway.

A broad-based movement of labour, indigenous peoples and university students responded to the threat in Cochabamba with four months of mass protests that culminated in the April "War for Water," a week-long struggle that used blockades, strikes and confrontational protests to effectively shut down the city of six-hundred thousand. As a result, the governor resigned after stating during a television broadcast that he did not want to take responsibility for the "blood bath" to follow. The Bolivian government declared a "state of emergency," arresting water-rights leaders, censoring the media and sending armed soldiers into the streets, resulting in one death and many injuries. Finally, on the night of April 10, the Bolivian government declared the contract void and met all of the demands of the protests. The people of Cochabamba won a historic victory! The people of Cochabamba have received widespread international support in their fight against the privatization of their water and the corporatization of their country. Since this victory, the Cochabamba Declaration has been signed by citizens, organizations and countries all over the world.

If governments decide to join the FTAA, water, as well as other public resources and institutions, will become a tradable commodity, and our rights to them will pass from the hands of citizens and national governments to those of corporations. It will undermine the work of communities in making resources available and institutions accessible to all people. It will also increase the inequality between the rich and the poor, between and within countries.

Water activists from Brazil and other Latin American countries spoke at the People's Summit, drawing attention to the issues affecting their own countries. As well, the "Living River" action in Québec City on Saturday, April 21, declared water to be sacred and vital to life on earth. It drew attention to the right to water for all people. The organizers of the action, eco-spiritual activists from North America, passed out information about the Cochabamba Declaration and stressed the connections between corporate globalization, environmental degradation and the lack of social justice.

The following declaration was written by water activists from Cochabamba and other international water activists attending a seminar on the global pressure to turn water over to private water corporations held in Cochabamba on December 8, 2000.

The Cochabamba Declaration

We, citizens of Bolivia, Canada, United States, India, Brazil:

Farmers, workers, indigenous people, students, professionals, environmentalists, educators, nongovernmental organizations, retired people, gather today in solidarity to combine forces in defense of the vital right to water.

Here, in this city which has been an inspiration to the world for its retaking of that right through civil action, courage and sacrifice, standing as heroes and heroines against corporate, institutional and governmental abuse, and trade agreements which destroy that right, in use of our freedom and dignity, we declare the following:

For the right to life, for the respect of nature and the uses and traditions of our ancestors and our peoples, for all time the following shall be declared as inviolable rights with regard to the uses of water given us by the earth:

1. Water belongs to the earth and all species and is sacred to life, therefore, the world's water must be conserved, reclaimed and protected for all future generations and its natural patterns respected.

2. Water is a fundamental human right and a public trust to be guarded by all levels of government, therefore, it should not be commodified, privatized or traded for commercial purposes. These rights must be enshrined at all levels of government. In particular, an international treaty must ensure these principles are noncontrovertable.

3. Water is best protected by local communities and citizens who must be respected as equal partners with governments in the protection and regulation of water. Peoples of the earth are the only vehicle to promote earth democracy and save water.

The Winnipeg kitchen's water cart was always a welcome sight. Not only did it keep the kitchen with a continuous supply of water, but it also refilled bottles at the various actions throughout the old city. (Photo: Emmie Tsumura)

Statement from Akwesasne Community Organizers[1]

Akwesasne Community Organizers

May 3, 2001

For Distribution:

We have lived the past 100 years under the Indian Acts of two colonial governments. For 100 years, we have endured the indignities of poverty, isolation, hunger and disease. For 100 years, we have been environmentally destroyed. Our women give birth to babies that suffer from the effects of pollution, children born without intestines or intestines that grow on the outside of their bodies. We are told that new mothers can no longer feed their newborns because of toxin levels within their bodies. For 100 years we have not been allowed to speak out for fear of reprisals from our own duly elected Indian Act governments.

On April 19th, we did something that this community has never seen before.

Prior to the arrival of the American Caravan, Akwesasne community people were told to stay indoors, not to let their children outside, and to prepare for the looting and burning of their homes. Band Council and other counter-intelligence organizations disseminated false information in an attempt to keep people out of our community, and to keep Mohawk people from participating in the realization that we share a common political struggle.

The overwhelming majority of community people understood the issue and were honored to have warriors from other nations coming into Akwesasne.

Despite local governments' hysteria, 80 people participated in cooking and organizing for the day. Two hundred and fifty people participated in the event by attending the feast, crossing the bridge or observing from behind customs lines. The Ontario Coalition Against Poverty helped us with organizing, but we stressed that it was something that must come from within the community. We planned the April 19th event with the intention of organizing our people, so that we could legitimately play a part in the plans to defeat the government. We acknowledge the mistakes we made in organizing; however, these tactical errors should not override the success of the day. We defeated the attempts of five governing bodies that were committed to stopping the event. We showed courage and integrity to the 13 policing agencies that had threatened to attack, beat or kill us and our families if we continued with our plans.

We met adversity with honor to the very end. Any shortfalls within the day are necessary to understand so that they do not appear in future issues, but clearly, we feel that this was an issue of the people of Akwesasne and we gauge our success on that. We have opened the door to building links with non-native people and organizations. We stood together to demonstrate to governments that they will no longer be able to isolate us from each other.

Your courage to overcome the political adversity surrounding the day will not be forgotten, and we can now legitimately work towards understanding your issues and having you understand ours.

　　We are not prepared to endure another 100 years.

Yours in solidarity,
Mohawk Organizers of Akwesasne

Note

1. This statement is posted on the Ontario Coalition Against Poverty (OCAP) website, *www.ocap.ca*.

(Photo: Brandon Constant)

Declaration of the Second Peoples' Summit

Delegates of the Second Peoples' Summit

Québec, April 19, 2001

No to the FTAA!
Another Americas is Possible!

We, the delegates of the Second Peoples' Summit of the Americas, declare our opposition to the Free Trade Area of the Americas (FTAA) project concocted secretly by the 34 Heads of State and government hand in hand with the American Business Forum.

Who are we? We are the Hemispheric Social Alliance, the voices of the unions, popular and environmental organisations, women's groups, human rights organisations, international solidarity groups, indigenous, peasant and student associations and church groups. We have come from every corner of the Americas to make our voices heard.

We reject this project of liberalised trade and investment, deregulation and privatization. This neo-liberal project is racist and sexist and destructive of the environment. We propose to build new ways of continental integration based on democracy, human rights, equality, solidarity, pluralism and respect for the environment.

Broken Promises

Since the 1994 Miami Summit, the Heads of State and government have committed themselves to reinforce democracy and human rights, to support education and to reduce poverty in the Americas. For seven years nothing has been done. The only issue that has moved forward, taking advantage of deficit in democracy, is the negotiation of the Free Trade Area of the Americas (FTAA).

This is not the first time that presidents and Heads of State have promised a better world. This is not the first time that the people of the Americas have been told to wait for the fruits of free trade to come. This is not the first time that we are forced to take note that the Heads of State have broken their promises.

The FTAA project is a charter of investors' rights and freedoms, sanctions the primacy of capital over labour, transforms life and the world into merchandise, negates human rights, sabotages democracy and undermines state sovereignty.

The Asymmetric Americas

Indeed, we live in an Americas marked by intolerable inequalities and unjustifiable political and economic asymmetries. Half of the population of 800 million, of whom almost 500 million are Latin American, live in poverty. The South has a debt of US$792 billion to the North, resulting in a debt servicing of US$123 billion in 1999 alone. Capital, technologies and patents are concentrated in the North. Canada and the U.S. hold 80 percent of the economic might. Many new jobs are in the informal sector, where labour rights are constantly flouted.

Free trade agreements aggravate inequalities between the rich and the poor, between men and women, between countries of the North and countries of the South, and destroy the ecological links between human beings and the environment. Twenty percent of the world population consumes 80 percent of the natural resources of the planet. These free trade agreements prioritize exports at the expense of the needs of local communities. We are witnessing the consolidation of economic and legal corporate power at the expense of popular sovereignty.

Free trade agreements favour the commodification of public goods and the planet (water, genetic heritage, etc.). The neo-liberal logic reduces the citizen to a mere consumer and ultimately to a product. It favours short term gains without considering the social and environmental cost of goods and services.

Under the pressure of large agribusinesses and dumping policies, free trade agreements threaten local small-scale agriculture, mostly performed by women, putting food security in danger.

Free trade agreements encourage the systematic privatisation of public goods such as health, education and social programs along with Structural Adjustment Programs in the South and budget cuts in the North. These agreements rely on women to take up the collective tasks now abandoned by the state.

Free trade agreements foster the marginalisation of indigenous people and the appropriation and subsequent marketing of their knowledge.

Free trade agreements lead to an increasing feminisation of poverty and an exacerbation of existing inequalities between men and women. For example, women get paid less, work in hard and often degrading conditions without union rights, undertake unpaid and unrecognised work for the family and community, suffer the commodification of their bodies—now the third most lucrative trafficking after drugs and arms—and are subjected to increased domestic violence and violation of their fundamental rights.

Free trade agreements are accompanied by the militarisation of entire societies through schemes such as Plan Colombia and are also related to arms trafficking.

There is no possible fair agreement in such a context.

What We Want

We want to build bridges between the peoples of the Americas, to draw on the pluralism of our histories and our cultures and to strengthen each other in the exercising of a representative and participatory democracy. We want to share the same passion for an absolute respect of human rights and the same commitment to have these rights respected. We want to live together in true equality between men and women, to take care of all our children and to share the wealth fairly and in solidarity.

We want complete respect for workers rights, trade union rights and collective bargaining.

We want to ensure the primacy of human rights and collective rights, as defined in international instruments, over commercial agreements.

We want states that promote the common good and that are able to intervene actively to ensure the respect of rights. We want states to strengthen democracy, to ensure the production and distribution of wealth, to guarantee universal and free access to quality public education, and to health care, particularly concerning women's reproductive rights. We want states to eliminate violence against women and children and to ensure respect for the environment on behalf of the current and future generations.

We want socially productive and ecologically responsible investment. The rules applied across the continent should encourage foreign investors who will guarantee the creation of quality jobs, sustainable production and economic stability, while blocking speculative investments.

We want fair trade.

We welcome the conclusions of the deliberations of the different forums in the Peoples' Summit. These reflections will be integrated into the Alternatives for the Americas document.

We call upon the peoples of the Americas to intensify their mobilisation to fight the FTAA project and to build other integration alternatives based on democracy, social justice and sustainable development.

Another Americas is possible!

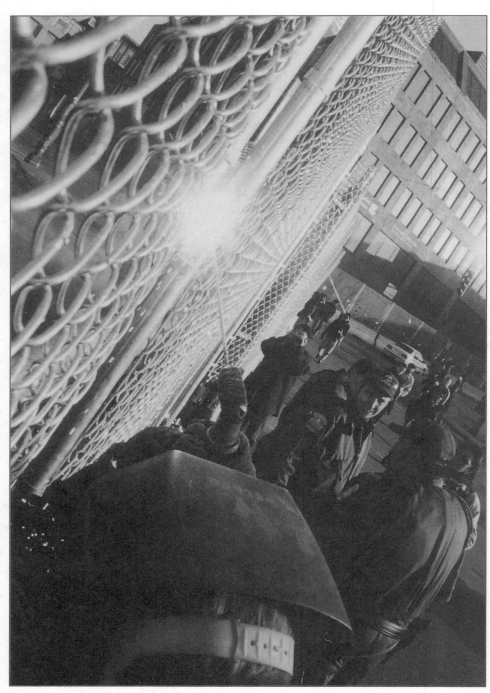

The security perimeter at Côte D'Abraham is welded and locked shut—an eerie prelude of events yet to come. (Photo: Steve Daniels)

The security perimeter, erected to protect the official summit participants, was originally sealed with a padlock. It was soon reinforced with a bulldozer, dozens of riot police, water cannons and tear gas. (Photo: Steve Daniels)

Protesters made themselves heard both with song and slogan. (Photo: Emmie Tsumura)

Students march to reinforce the need for strongly supported public education. (Photo: Erin George)

from the front:
accounts from Québec City

First We Took Québec City, Then Drummondville: The True Story Behind the Anarchist Invasion of Québec City

Norman Nawrocki

Official Anarchist Storyteller,
Montréal, April 18, 2001

It's taken us years of hard work, but finally, we, the anarchists of the world, members of the 10-million-strong, glorious, international "Black Wedge," will see anarchy in Québec City, thanks in no small part to the cooperation of the state, the CSIS, the RCMP and, of course, the dedicated journalists of the mass media who unknowingly helped us unfold our ingenious, five-stage Secret Master Plan for Total World Social Revolution!

The Facts

- It's official. We convinced the authorities a long time ago to hold the Summit of the Americas in Québec City—a city of 500,000 closet anarchists—and to call this summit the FTAA, which really means "Fantastic Times for Anarchist Activists."
- We arranged for a minor earthquake in Seattle, power blackouts in California and a few natural disasters around the world to show that we don't fool around. We are serious. We can cause major disruptions and bad cable television reception.
- We infiltrated global secret police forces to put the fear of *anarchy* in them, to convince them that the threat of anarchism is very real.

> The RCMP are certainly worried. The presence of anarchists in Québec is one of the top reasons for the 6,000 police officers, the arsenal of plastic bullets and the 3.8 metre-high security fence, nicknamed The Wall. (*Montreal Gazette*, April 13, 2001)

Since this report, we learned that an additional 1200 Canadian soldiers and innumerable American military personnel will also be present to counter our presence. We arranged that too.

- We recruited the Québec premier, Bernard Landry, as one of our top secret agents and turned his party, the annoying Parti Québécois, into a front for the anarchist Black Bloc.
- We convinced them to build the formidable, four-kilometre-long "Wall of Shame." This wall will now help us contain, secure and imprison all the despised members of this hemisphere's ruling class while we execute our plan: to turn Québec City into a truly

independent anarchist communist paradise with no more bosses, borders or rulers. We'll transform it into a self-managed, totally liberated zone, where we will socialize everything, feed and house everyone and launch a staging ground to help us further our dream for global social revolution.

How We Will Do This:

It's simple. While most of our people—local, Québec City resident, anarchist Black Bloc card-carrying members—are securing the enormous free zone outside the walled off security perimeter, the rest of us will immobilize and apprehend the trapped members of the despised ruling class and their thousands of lackeys and armed bodyguards.

We know the authorities are terrified and are trying to play down the extent of our operation and our invasion force. Contrary to an unsubstantiated CSIS report that some members of the anti-capitalist convergence, the CLAC, may be bringing explosives to Québec City, the truth is infinitely more interesting.

1. Approximately three million members of CLAC are already camped out in non-descript RVs in Québec City suburbs, each heavily armed with stink bombs, exploding Cuban cigars and Barbra Streisand albums;

2. Among them, an international contingent of 30,000 anarchist ninja warriors are preparing to breach the security fence at dawn to clear landing pads for several hundred anarchist Black Cross helicopters carrying 14,000 Belgian anarchist pie-throwing specialists;

3. This manoeuvre will provide cover for the Brazilian Anarchist Air Force crop-dusting jets, primed to drop five tons of Ecstasy over the target area;

4. While the Ecstasy falls, ten thousand three-headed anarchist aliens from Mars—disguised as visiting space doughnut entrepreneurs—will sneak past security checkpoints and proceed to vaporize all FTAA summit meeting places, including all local MacDonald's, Burger King and Harvey's outlets;

5. At this exact moment, 25,000 screaming American anarchist kindergarten kids will spontaneously pop out of city manholes armed with vicious Pickachoo Warriors, and swarm any un-drugged summit security forces and drag them back into the sewers;

6. Already, the entire official Summit Translation Corps has been infiltrated by Italian anarchist surrealist translators preparing to insult every summit delegate;

7.   If any delegates survive this, they won't survive the food, since the official catering staff has been infiltrated by anarchist "food not bombs" chefs, who plan to lace every dish with laxatives and sprinkle itching powder on all the toilet paper;

8.   All the moaning and groaning members of the despised ruling class will then be hog-tied together with a huge anarchist black bungee cord, suspended and bounced from the peak of the Chateau Frontenac and forced to listen to the songs of long-time anarchist cheerleader mom Céline Dion;

9.   At some point, a giant inflated Trojan condom will appear over the City and parachute a 300,000 strong, trained anti-terrorist anarchist peacekeeping force to secure the ground and prevent any dangerous and violent blue bloc CIA, FBI and RCMP agents from interfering with the festive, anarchist Carnival Against Capitalism;

10. Further support will be provided by the Russian Anarchist Black Submarine Fleet patrolling the St. Lawrence River with anarchist good humour laughing gas missiles;

11. If we anarchists encounter any remaining resistance, Anarchist Starfleet Command will be positioned over Québec with a giant anti-Viagra stun ray.

A Hollywood version of "The Anarchist Take Over of Québec City," starring Ben Affleck and Julia Roberts as love-struck members of the Black Bloc, is already being filmed on the spot. The story will also appear as a new Harry Potter novel. We've been promised that anarcho Christians will rewrite it into their newest version of the Bible. And finally, a long-awaited video game of the impending, epic, anarchist victory will be out shortly.

Open. A shop owner invites patrons while preparing for the worst. (Photo: Steve Daniels)

A passer-by pauses to comprehend the signs indicating a pre-summit liquidation sale. (Photo: Steve Daniels)

A Québec City Diary

Philippe de Grosbois

Thursday, April 19

My fourth day in Québec City began with a walk to find out where the anti-genetically modified organisms (GMO) picnic was taking place. I thought it was at the Plains of Abraham but finally realized it was in front of the Québec Ministry of Agriculture building.

Before I got there, I ended up walking downtown alone, near the infamous perimeter. It was surreal…. I walked past cops ready for combat, fully dressed in riot gear.

I finally met some people I knew and we walked down to the picnic. The food was great and there were at least two hundred people. During our lunch, the "velorutionary bikesheviks" arrived at the ministry. There were thirty-four bikers, and all seemed to be in high spirits, a little relieved finally to be in Québec.

A few decent speakers followed, and then it was José Bové's turn. I'm usually not big on "stars," but I have to say that his celebrity doesn't seem to have gone to his head. Bové, who became renowned in 1999 for his involvement in bulldozing a McDonald's restaurant under construction, encouraged people during his talk at the people's summit to tear transgenic plants out of the soil, to label GMO products on store shelves and "not to hesitate to act illegally."

After his encouraging presentation, a journalist from the *Ottawa Citizen* asked my friend Marie and I what we thought of someone making a call to act illegally. I answered, sarcastically, that I found his behaviour scandalous, and she turned away to interview my friend. I couldn't believe it. Her question was so useless, especially after everything Bové had said about the patenting of plants and eventually animals, and some day, maybe even humans. The mainstream media is only out to make headlines, not to cover the issues.

Later in the afternoon, we went to a joint press conference being held by six different groups. Among them were the CLAC and CASA, OQP2001 and the International Socialists. It was a sort of common front against the FTAA. The diversity of groups coming together made it a major political breakthrough. Journalists were once again focusing mostly on the supposed violent/non-violent division. It was revolting. I left feeling dejected and thinking that the mass media was worthless. On our way out we grabbed some pamphlets to hand out at shopping malls. Five of us went to the Place Ste-Foy in suburban Québec, only to be denied entry to the mall by security guards wrongfully thinking they were CIA agents.

Security at the neighbouring shopping centre, Place de la Cité, acted quite differently and had no problems with us passing out information. Everything we had brought was written with nonactivists in mind. One pamphlet used a "fishing" metaphor in its basic explanation of the FTAA. People were generally very receptive. This is the kind of literature we must produce more often. We really need to reach out to workers and consumers, an effort that I think is really lacking right now. Afterwards, I went to the CASA/CLAC spokescouncil meeting at the University of Laval, where there was lots of talk about blocking the three main access points to the summit. It was encouraging!

After dinner, at 8pm, the Torchlight March began. It was the first large-scale protest, the first test. I was a little nervous and brought along all my gear: raincoat, ski goggles, masks, camera. In theory, most of it wouldn't be needed since it was a "green" action, but you never know.

To most people's surprise, the march went off without a hitch. It was a peaceful yet defiant march. And it was strange to see so little police presence. I've seen the same number of cops at Montréal rallies with three hundred people. There had to be at least two thousand people at this one. It was actually really nice walking through the suburbs. Everyone continuously tried to invite people to join the march.

The only problem with the march was its length. Two hours of solid walking was tiring. We went all the way to l'Ilôt Fleuri, a large urban space under overpasses, full of beautiful works of art. It lent an interesting ambiance, all these people in an underground place.... There was music, a concert-like rave. CASA/CLAC's cultural committee really came out strong. The sound was great. It was a fun party!

Friday, April 20

This day is when the action really began. I went to Laval to meet some friends from Montréal. They had slept at the university's athletic complex, as had thousands of other people from all over the continent. There were two protests leaving the university nearly simultaneously. The first was organized by the anti-FTAA GOMM and was to be mostly a green-yellow action. The other, organized by CLAC, was yellow-red.

Finally, after nearly two hours of waiting, both marches began and it was a really bizarre scene. At the next street corner, there were people who were yelling into megaphones: "To go with GOMM, go left; for the CLAC go right." It's hard to say how many people went either way. It was about 60 percent CLAC, 40 percent GOMM. Regardless, these were two very big marches.

Thus we began another long march, from the university to the perimeter at René-Lévesque. It was a great march. There were probably close to ten thousand people. There was a Statue of Liberty on stilts, countless giant puppets, rhythmic drumming and lots of smiles. The Radical Cheerleaders were there, and so were the Raging Grannies and the "Black Bloc." It was in the post-Seattle tradition of decentralized protests, minus any large union presence. At some points, we could see the other march running parallel to us but more to the north. It was exciting! Once near the downtown area, there was a call: "Green to the left along St-Jean, yellow straight ahead, towards the perimeter." We went straight ahead.

Finally at 3pm we arrived at the end of the march. There were thousands of people at the perimeter. We were told that parts of the wall had come down. The tear gas began to fly. We walked around a little near the perimeter. About thirty police advanced methodically towards us, and we began to retreat. Our multiple attempts to avoid the tear gas divided us. I was left with only one friend. We couldn't lose each other! Two white, military-type armoured vehicles with "Police" written on their sides arrived behind us. The water cannons were here. I found out afterwards that some people kicked the vehicles' windows in, forcing them to retreat after only a couple of pitiful attempts at spraying people.

The confrontation would last several hours. We went down to Rue St-Jean to rest and regroup. When we returned, this time we dared not leave, even if the police began to make advances, because the yellow zone helped to support the red. My mask and my ski goggles really helped.

We finally left at around 7pm, after almost seven hours of action. A couple of us walked all the way back to the university, the entire route reversed. From there, after much discussion, we went to have a beer. When we heard that there were still demonstrations going on at around 10:30pm, we wanted to go, but eventually fatigue set in and we just went to sleep.

Breaching the wall was certainly a symbolic victory. But, in reality, we must keep in mind that we are no longer able to have our voices heard by delegates and no longer capable of blocking their meetings.

Despite this, these two days (April 19 and 20), the dates of two important CLAC actions, proved to me that respecting a diversity of tactics really can work well. The green remained pretty darned green, with regard to militant action and arrests (obviously, safety could not be completely guaranteed: some green zones were targeted by loads of gas, among other things). The yellow and red were fairly well divided. We knew what we were to do, and there was a lot of support between the two groups. One did risky actions for the other (breaches in the wall, for example), the other attracted a large number of people. It really did work well!

Saturday, April 21

We woke from a semi-rejuvenating sleep. It was cold, and I realized one hour after I woke up that my ankles and calves had begun to hurt. After eating breakfast, we went by taxi to the Old Port for the Peoples' March. There were already enormous amounts of people there, and people kept arriving. I saw the people from the CLAC with their van.

I was looking forward to this march quite a bit. It was a really good idea to have an anti-capitalist contingent. For me, it was an occasion to publicly demonstrate my anti-capitalist convictions. And I found it important to diffuse the message from the grassroots, to the workers, to the many members of the many groups present.

The march began fairly slowly (tens of thousands of people creates slow traffic). It was very hot. I distributed material explaining the CLAC's anti-capitalist stance. In one part of the street, people started to see rising gas vapours in the distance. I sensed that this dampened spirits. Not long afterwards, the tension rose strangely. Gas vapours began to hit the demonstration, which was along Boulevard Charest. Most people were not prepared, including me. Everything was in my bag.

At the corner of Charest and Couronne, there was an invitation to branch off and go up towards the fence. I think that many people wanted to go, but they were neither physically nor psychologically ready to confront the police and their tear gas. I chose to go up. I had known for a while that I was going to. Exit the gentle march, which ended in the middle of nowhere. I returned to the ambiance of civil unrest. After a little while, I found my friends from the University of Québec at Montréal (UQAM), not too far from yesterday's location, near the Grand Théâtre.

These summits make for strange situations. There is the "spectacle" of revolution, not revolution itself. The spectacle makes a whirlwind tour from city to city, from Seattle to Washington, to Prague and Québec. Everybody tastes their own "piece of the spectacle," but the real uprising remains to be seen. I believe that this real uprising is the "movement's" biggest challenge, a bigger challenge than overcoming its supposed decentralized and heterogeneous character. We must evolve beyond the three-day revolution—the insurrectionist trip taken by those who can most afford it because they might never see anything more—to produce a real social movement.

Our group had an abrupt change in plans early in the evening. Most went out for dinner; half to a restaurant, the other half to a green zone nearby. I remained outside. By about 7pm, most had finished the meal and were waiting on the sidewalk when four police vehicles screeched to a halt and completely surrounded us. I stiffened.

I found out later that three of my friends had been arrested. One had gone back into the restaurant, but they followed him inside. They tried to grab two others, but one ran away; the other was asked lots of questions and then let go. It all took less than a minute, and then the police officers were gone as fast as they had arrived.

We were completely in shock. We all found ourselves back on the sidewalk in front of the restaurant. After talking for a little while, we finally decided to walk back towards the university. We were all very stressed, terrorized. We tried walking quickly and slowly, we yelled at those who were walking too far ahead, we tried to stay together. We couldn't understand why they had targeted our group.

Many of us took the bus back to Laval, where the legal collective had an office. We spoke to them and it helped us to relax. We thought we should write a communiqué. We had already heard about other kidnappings, including one in which the cops went into a convenience store, locked the doors and pointed out the arrestees. They had also busted the medical centre at gunpoint and gassed the Indymedia centre. We felt that we ought to describe the omnipresent state of terror.

Finally, we drove to our friend's apartment where several others from our group were staying. Everyone in the car was tense. We felt like we lived in a dictatorship with state surveillance, targeted arrests.... It was after 11pm when we arrived. Everyone was keeping quiet, whispering hellos, walking tip-toed, staying put. We were doing everything we could to avoid attracting attention from the neighbours, and possibly the police.

We at once realized the power of a totalitarian system. Fear and police power were controlling our movements, our speech, our actions. We were not used to this sort of police behaviour. We still found it in our ourselves to laugh, but we were terrorized.

It was a long and difficult night. We listened to a mainstream radio station's live account of the events throughout the night. They called it a riot. It was strange. It was like we were listening to a hockey game.

Around 3am we heard loud explosions downtown. The lights in the house dimmed down before each explosion, like in a power outage. After that we would hear a loud "Bang!" We found out later that it was the sound of exploding propane tanks thrown into a fire. There were maybe four or five of these explosions. It sounded like the end had come.

I finally went to sleep at 4:30am, like most of the group. I slept lightly, only managing to doze for a few hours. I was afraid the police would come knocking at the door, would make their way up to arrest us all, in this night of paranoia.

Sunday, April 22

We all woke up calmer. I was thinking only about making my way back to Montréal. I remember thinking to myself, "Once we're on the highway, far from Québec, everything will be better."

Before we left, we went up to the University of Laval for a press conference held by the legal collective—there had been over two hundred arrests the night before. But from the car, we saw lots of police vehicles in the parking lot and at the entrance. I was afraid that it might be a police raid of the area, so we continued without getting out of the car.

It all ended much more dismally than I had imagined. We hadn't taken the situation seriously enough in our preparations. Police repression and surveillance is extremely serious. Regardless, I'm happy I experienced what I did. On top of this, our three kidnapped friends were released a day later. Two of them had all their charges dropped, while the other still faces dubious charges.

I had expected that I would be more enthusiastic in Québec, more excited, since I had been looking forward to it for over a year. I now realize the limits of such mass actions. I think we have lots of work to do before we truly have a large, diverse and strong movement.

At the same time, I found it all very beautiful—all these ideas, all these groups, all these alliances. And in my opinion, the CLAC gained a lot of respect from groups throughout the Americas. We had not done any major actions since our birth a year before. I think we were ready for this one, and it showed. There were lots of people out at the actions, and the idea of respecting a diversity of tactics generally worked very well.

One such tactic was the idea of having American and Caribbean-wide day-long general strikes against the FTAA. Organizing such events would be quite a challenge, but could be an important step in building a global movement against capitalism. And we have four years to work out the details. This kind of organizing could go a long way to help the movement in becoming sustainable and eventually get out of the summit-hopping mentality. I now have hope.

Children add their voice to the many that would soon gather in Québec City. (Photo: Steve Daniels)

The bikesheviks arrive from Montréal. (Photo: Kevin Walsh)

Street performers take advantage of a roadside billboard. (Photo: Leslie Menagh)

A Kiss for the Riot Cop

Sandra Alland

Last night I kissed
a riot cop

or I would have

if I could've gotten over
the 20-foot wall 4 concrete barriers
past rubber bullet guns tear gas fumes
pepper spray plastic shields water cannons
masks horses pistols fists

But I did blow him a kiss

and he felt it

I saw him flinch
in recognition.

A view from the outsite. Police were never far from the fence. (Photo: Emmie Tsumura)

Anishinaabe Girl in Québec

Jennifer Bennett (Wikwemikong Band, Wikwemikong, Ontario)

The best vacation of my life began Wednesday night, April 18, 2001, at 10pm, the day after my twenty-third birthday. I hopped on a bus with about fifty other Hamilton folks, most of whom were McMaster University students. I recognized the majority of the faces on the bus and was mildly amused by the idea that no matter our stance, the media would focus on the antagonistic constituent during the protests, overlooking the gentle-hearted smiles of these gentle souls who know that a peaceful, harmonic and just society requires a non-violent revolution, or dare I say, a non-violent evolution. I doubt that most of them had a speck of will to harm a fly.

The bus trip was organized by two dedicated organizers of the non-violent-oriented Hamilton Action for Social Change. After a few ironic stops at McDonald's in the middle of the night, we arrived in Québec around 8am on Thursday morning. I spent the morning making a banner I planned to carry for the Peoples' March on Saturday. Its simple design expressed my unspecified standpoint on the Free Trade Area of the Americas and its effect on Native people.

I knew that it was important for the world to know that an *Anishinaabe kwe* (Ojibwe woman) was present at and active in the FTAA protest; part of the specific brand of racism hurled at Indians is the extreme marginalization of our people onto reserve(ation)s in the middle of nowhere. In my own experience growing up in Florida, most people thought that Native people were extinct. Outta sight, outta mind, I guess. I also felt it necessary to show solidarity with indigenous peoples in Central and South America as well as Mexico, to let them know that they had a cousin up here who knew about their plight and was ready to express her dismay and outrage to the powers that be.

My banner also symbolized my heartache at the condition of reserve(ation) life in our industrialized countries of Canada and the U.S.—the very countries that were leading this summit and whose hands were still crusted with dried blood from the violent, genocidal domestic history with Native peoples. And now these same countries were salivating as they gazed hungrily to the South. So, as a symbol of my solidarity, I made a huge circle of four felt pieces in the traditional colours: red, black, yellow and white; and very simply, underneath, I wrote, "End Oppression for Native People."

That afternoon, we acquainted ourselves with this astonishingly beautiful city, in small groups as curious friends would—not quite as "affinity" groups. And we absolutely *had* to get a glimpse of the infamous wall. I was revelling in the culture. I felt that it was as close to Europe as I'd ever been. The architecture was so foreign and I googled over the desserts in a small *boulangerie* (bakery) where we stopped during our tour of *le mur* (the wall). Near a touristy section of town, my friends asked a bullet-proof-vested RCMP officer behind the wall what would happen if one of us were to be caught on the other side without a residency pass. And more to the point, they asked under what type of legislation could they pull off this amazing feat of antagonism and apparent violation of civil rights. Having grown up in the U.S., where police violence is quite the norm, I was shocked when they ended up extracting a very casual exchange from him. This really is Canada, eh?

Not more than a few hundred metres down from the *boulangerie*, a section of the wall was riddled with dozens of balloons, streamers and construction paper flowers with French-language messages like peace, equality, democracy, social justice, human rights. Amidst these decorations we saw yet another symbol of the amazing positivity, creativity and humour of those in the movement. There, attached to the fence, was a sign in French that read "Thank you for not feeding the animals."

Later Thursday evening, my friends and my women-friends caught up with the end of the Women's March, "Weaving the Web of Resistance." I understood it to be a pagan-based ceremony and rally during which women from the U.S. and Canada had woven spider webs of ribbons and cloth and adorned them with trinkets and pictures and other small objects. The idea was to transform the wall into a positive protective force for the protesters by placing these webs on the security perimeter. We joined the last stretch of the march, parading up Boulevard René-Lévesque to a main entrance to the security zone, which later became the site of the major conflicts.

As I ran up to join the march, I almost stopped dead in my tracks when, much to my surprise and chagrin, a woman right next to me, with a ridiculous smile on her face, said, "Isn't our Goddess awesome? She's so beautiful!" She was referring to the effigy leading the march. It was clad in a paisley purple skirt and loose green top, painted with pink-apricot skin and freckles, and draped with strips of orange and red cloth for hair. Goddess? Goddess?!? So even the Goddess is white, huh? Yet another symbol of power painfully bleaching my skin and hair. And in the midst of my shock, looking for someone else who could be feeling the same pangs of exclusion, I couldn't help but notice that I was having a hard time seeing more women of colour at the march than I could count on one hand. I didn't ask myself why because the answer was painfully obvious to me and so, defeated, I swallowed my insult and danced with my "fellow" women nonetheless. I didn't realize at the time that it would be the most quiescent and peaceful demonstration of the entire weekend.

Later that evening, my friends and I were guided to a place called l'Ilôt Fleurie, which I referred to as the "Alice-in-Wonderland playground." Tucked underneath ribbons of overpasses, l'Ilôt Fleurie was defined by a kaleidoscope of jaw-dropping graffiti painted on the side walls of ramps and columns. Scattered around its perimeter was a menagerie of gargantuan sculptures. There was a stage for musicians in one corner and a couple of fire barrels to give warmth to the wanderers who found themselves there. While getting a bite to eat at the free food kitchen and warming up by a fire at this safe zone for protesters, I made conversation with a local Québécois, who to my surprise and disappointment had never before heard of

Ojibwes. In fact, he told me that most people from the area didn't know much about *les autochtones* (Native peoples). But in a cultural exchange, he offered to take me around the parts of the city that were still accessible to me the following day and I told him more about Native history and culture. Hey, I even learned how to pronounce *autochtones* correctly.

On Friday I missed the majority of the peaceful CLAC march from the University of Laval to the wall, nearly four kilometres down Boulevard René-Lévesque, but I caught up with it just as it reached *le mur*. My curiosity led me to the frontlines to observe, and I didn't realize that I had wandered into the middle of the red zone (a risk-arrest area). As I looked up to my left at the apartment building just off the street and wondered what the elderly observers standing on their porches were thinking about this whole spectacle, I noticed the weekend's first puffs of tear gas. I smiled as the police began to hurl canisters of tear gas into the frontlines of demonstrators, only to have the forty-kilometre winds blow it right back down on them. After a section of the fence came down, cheers went through the crowd.

I think this was a turning point in the police reaction to our presence. They began loading canisters into a gun, projecting the tear gas further into the crowd. I found out later that their restraint, for which they were commended by Prime Minister Chrétien, flew out the window as the weekend progressed. The police began to aim their guns at protesters, sometimes at distances of only ten metres. One man suffered a broken arm when he was struck by a launched tear-gas canister. Despite police efforts, the winds still carried the gas away from us back onto the police. I watched happily as some protesters picked up canisters and threw them back at the fence. I didn't have my vinegar-soaked hankie or any eye protection but thought that I could always retreat if things got bad, so I continued to watch the clash unfurl as the tension in the air intensified. Those who had been on the frontlines when the first of the tear gas was released were now running back into the crowd to get treated by medics with water or a neutralizing solution. A few were treated right next to my feet, and tears swelled in my eyes listening to their cries of pain—on their knees, faces flushed, noses running and eyes swollen shut.

When I decided I had witnessed enough chaos, I began to retreat but was cut off by two police vehicles, each armed with a mechanical fire hose on its hood, like a zit with a vengeance. The crowd quickly parted as the trucks blared through the rear of the crowd. And then, in one of the most amazing acts of bravery that I witnessed that weekend, one man, completely alone, walked right up to the first truck with a white sheet tied to a tree branch that read "*democratie,*" and he planted his sign in the nozzle. The crowd must have held its breath for a full sixty seconds while we digested what we saw. He *stopped* it. He *stopped* the truck. After a few eternal seconds, people nearby scurried up behind him, starting a tidal wave of people that forced the truck to retreat. The crowd chased the trucks back, but the police insisted on mowing down two dozen retreating protesters with a cannon blast of water in five degree weather and fierce winds.

I thought the trucks marked the end of the rear attack, but the police finally figured out how to use the wind to their benefit and released the tear gas at our backs. I began to gag. My eyes began to burn and my lungs began to scream. I was choking on fire. I dug frantically in my pack until I remembered that I had left my handkerchief at my dorm that morning. My friend and I skipped behind a building in a meagre attempt to get out of the noxious wind. I was worried that, if in my retreat I came near the police, I would be arrested because they had moved out from behind the perimeter and were snatching solitary demonstrators. They even began blocking off the side streets that would have served as exit routes for us, funnelling the crowd in one direction—away from the wall and into the midst of the tear gas.

When I realized that my eyes were getting worse and I could no longer open them, I frantically tried to rinse them out. I discovered that, besides the effects on the throat and eyes, tear gas reacts with water on human skin to burn like hell. A litre of water later, the burning finally left me. Two elderly adults came up to me with palms outstretched, begging for water to rinse out their eyes. What I thought was supposed to be a peaceful solidarity march turned into a battlefield. Locals, peaceful marchers and police were caught with me in the middle of it, and tear gas does not discriminate among its victims.

Later, as I was relaxing in a pizza joint near CEGEP Limoilou where I was staying, I was surprised to find that most locals responded to my questions with, "You want answer in Spanish?" I had hoped that my abalone shell earrings and my shirt that read "North American Indian Immigration Officer ON DUTY" would have tipped them off that I was not Latina, but *une autochtonne. C'est la vie*, I guess.

I was in the middle of eating my pizza when I had a tear gas relapse in my right eye. It was, oddly enough, more painful than the first time around. When I noticed my eye beginning to swell up in a matter of seconds, I abandoned any cultural sensitivity I might have had. The people at the bar, understandably, ignored my initial pleas in English to direct me to the bathroom, and I was near screaming when it came back to me, "*Où est la toilette?*" Lucky for me, a fellow anglophone protester, who was in the bathroom, recognized what was happening to me and guided me outside for fresh air and a more vigorous treatment. I became a spectacle for passersby and the folks in the pizza joint as I knelt at the corner of an intersection with four wonderfully gracious women surrounding me, treating my eyes with Rolaids water. They kindly walked me back to CEGEP Limoilou. The woman who had helped me in the bathroom also tried to get the rest of my dinner wrapped to go but, in the linguistic confusion, the waiter tossed it in the trash. When it rains, it pours.

Saturday, during the Peoples' March, I carried my banner with a friend, sporting my favourite pair of abalone shell earrings and a T-shirt my father gave me that had a Tommy Hilfiger symbol and the caption "Anishinaabe Girl" in lieu of "Tommy Girl." The Aboriginal Peoples Television Network easily spotted me and stopped me for an interview. I had spent the majority of the march next to a group of beautiful young people clad in blue jumpsuits with a design on the back reading "Western Massachusetts Revolutionary Drumcore" and pounding out complex, groovalicious dances on snares, buckets, cymbals and a big bass drum.

I was left with a complete inability to articulate my thought processes. I left the interview embarrassed, knowing that I must have sounded like Beavis and Butt-head ... huh-huh-uhhh-huh-huh words ... huh-words uh-words.... I found out later that my fumbling thoughts disqualified me from getting a sound bite, but at least I got my face and banner on the screen. One of the Native reporters asked, "So, how does it feel to be the only Aboriginal person at this march?" Shocked for the thirty-seventh time that weekend, gawking at his cynicism for a few moments, scratching my head and thinking it hard to believe that in the group of fifty thousand I could be the only one from a First Nation in Canada or the Americas for that matter, I could only say, "Somebody's gotta do it."

I have plans to return to the city in the future when I can be a regular tourist and visit the plethora *des musées, des parcs,* et *des places touristiques*[1] without that ridiculous wall. Even though thirty-four delegates signed that disgusting piece of paper, I know the struggle is far from over. I can still feel that uplifting, enlightening and gloriously inspirational high of marching with fifty thousand well-educated, creative and beautiful people from all over the world to express our right to dissent from those who would put *l'argent avant les gens.*[2]

★   I would like to extend my sincerest, heart-felt "chi miigwetch" (Thank you/Merci beaucoup) to all of the countless, beautiful student volunteers at CEGEP Limoilou for going to such selfless, tremendous lengths to provide an impenetrable safe haven for me and my friends during the summit.

Notes

1. Museums, parks and tourist spots.
2. Profits before people.

Dragonflies dance above the crowd of marchers heading to the perimeter. (Photo: Steve Daniels)

Green-zone activists dance and celebrate as a form of protest. This location would be heavily tear gassed before the end of the summit. (Photo: Emmie Tsumura)

Double Agent Dey
Sujata Dey

It was the middle of April when I heard about the National Campus Community Radio Association (NCRA) press passes. Eight lucky community journalists would have the chance to cover the upcoming Summit of the Americas in Québec City. I thought it would be a great opportunity to do some advocacy journalism: stir up shit and find the stories hidden under all the summit rhetoric.

Of course, I thought there wouldn't be much violence, maybe a little pepper spray, a little back and forth scuffles between cops and protesters. I was not prepared in any way for the confrontations that happened. This is Canada. Things like that don't happen here, I thought. I knew the police were going to be overzealous and were probably involved in a little pre-summit espionage, but things would go as we expect them to in Canada. That's exactly what I told the CBC report before I left: *"Il n'y aura pas de violence à Québec,"* I said, convinced. In other words, I was extremely naïve.

Accommodation was sort of second on my priority list. Late in the game, I had no idea if I had even been accredited. In fact, I was already in Québec when I actually knew that I would be allowed into the summit. From Day One, the independent media were going to be at a disadvantage. The mainstream media outlets had been on alert for a few months. We had less than a week to prepare for one of the biggest events in recent Canadian history. They had cell phones, laptops, expense accounts, satellites and live broadcast dishes. We had … well, I did have a calling card. As for accommodation, I thought fate would provide. As we got closer to the summit, I realized I was going to have to deal with the fact that the only thing I was going to get was a place on the floor at the University of Laval. I could book a room at the Holiday Inn where a lot of the journalists and delegates with smaller expense accounts were, but I really couldn't afford it.

From attending conferences in the past, I knew that everyone would be in their pressed suits, fresh and relaxed with specific agendas in mind. I imagined that my friend and I were going to be greasy, unwashed, tired journalists entering their private little party.

So how does the fashion-conscious activist/journalist prepare both for the oh-so-chic world of an anarchist community and for dining with the suits? I think the following shopping list contains the must-haves for anyone trying to cover a major summit while camping: makeup; utility pants (army fatigues); blow dryer; wet naps (in case there is no shower access); iron; earplugs (to actually get sleep); suit; bike lock; cell phone/mini disc recorder; t-shirts with activist slogans to sleep in (just so no one thinks you're infiltrating). Going between worlds became this startling exercise in culture shock. I felt like a spy going behind enemy lines during a war. As an activist without a press pass, the police would look at me as the enemy. Just asking for directions became an exercise in intimidation. The police grabbed our maps and looked us up and down when we asked them. But then, even though the woman at the press booth was quite confused about how I could be from Canada with a name like mine ("No, but what country are you from?"), I did end up getting my press pass. I got accreditation. It was time to join the fraternity. From now on police officers would pat me on the back when they escorted me across the lines. They would say "hello" when they saw my pass.

On the first day, I attempted to cross the perimeter. Walking up Côte d'Abraham, I started asking security people where the entrance was, half expecting them not to know. "Just that way," said the firefighter-turned-security. He looked at my media pass, "You better hide that. What if the *manifestants* (activists) see that?"

I passed. No one knew that only five minutes ago I was with my friends, the *manisfestants*. Activist journalism was about to begin.

I approached the fence. Later, I was to learn that it was the section of the fence that was first brought down. In Québec, the fence was so symbolic, dividing up worlds and instilling fear. Afterwards, when I returned home to Montréal and saw a fence, I automatically felt afraid, expecting someone to jump out and tell me which side of the fence I should be on.

I remember the first day I crossed the much-maligned perimeter. There were flowers and toilet paper wrapped around the fence. Outside there was celebration, protest, people, noise and humanity. People were emotionally charged, connected by their common experience of being targeted by the police. They were my heroes.

Inside the fence, the first thing I remember seeing is a bird. The world was silent except for the very distant sound of helicopters and sirens. Every few metres groups of police officers looked everyone up and down like pit bulls ready to strike. With very few people left, and with the police and the cobblestone streets, it felt like I was in a European village during the Second World War. In fact, the city was being occupied.

The first thing to remember in a state of occupation is that there is no such thing as reliable information. Outside, rumors flew. "Someone was killed. They are going to turn off all cell phones." Some of it was warranted. E-mails arrived mysteriously late. Cell phones would stop working. On the inside of the wall, all we heard was "I don't know."

Most reporters were in the Congress Centre, where the temporary press centre was set up. Most were complaining about the situation. "Where is the press conference? I don't know. What's going on today? I don't know. Which way to the bus? I don't know. Could I speak to so and so? I don't know."

The summit was like Campbell's soup: sealed and pre-packaged. To this day, I don't actually know if there was a summit going on. It might as well have been coming from a sound stage in another room. It was so rehearsed and so inaccessible to us. Most of the summit's important events were closed to the media. The few events and photo opportunities available were open only to media pools, which meant that only a fraction of the thousand or so journalists could attend. As a reporter from a community radio station, I didn't have much of a chance of getting into these events.

But I did see a lot of these events on television in the Congress Centre: Aline Chrétien at the taffy pull with the other spouses, Jean Chrétien at the Inuit art exhibit. Leaders came in through underground parking garages from sealed cars to sealed buildings within sealed perimeters. In the Congress Centre, it was like living in the suburbs; lots of phones, television to watch, people to joke with and nothing to do. Many journalists inside complained that there wasn't really a story at all.

But with my nose for news, my talent for getting the story, I was going to proceed. Determination would not stop the fourth estate. I was going to go to the Peoples' Summit and then return to the official summit to get a response from the organizers about why the people were not allowed in. At this point I walked out of the building and got locked outside of the perimeter.

I spun around. I was told that, inside the perimeter, journalists were being locked in the Congress Centre, perhaps for the night. Some of my co-reporters had been tear gassed, along with other journalists who were inside the perimeter but downwind from the police. Everyone was getting tear gassed: prominent politicians, journalists, activists and passers-by. People were tear gassed for putting up banners, for daring to walk in the area, for standing their ground. That night, I went to a local bar where I saw some of the "violent" anarchists watching themselves on television, storming the fence. Someone passed around a rubber bullet. We were now hearing about arrests.

The next morning we ate the vegan meal provided by the People's Potato at Laval. Laval was starting to smell like tear gas. My colleague and I, broke and without an affinity group, decided to get back inside the perimeter. After all, I hadn't packed for tear gas. But this time, we weren't going to be nice. We dropped our "high level journalistic operation" and decided that there were tons of people covering the "outside" and that since there was nothing to cover on the "inside," we were going to be rowdy. We were going to remind people of what was going on outside.

The area was again filled with tear gas fumes. But the usual suspects were there: Don Newman, Mike Duffy, Jason Moscovitz. We rubbed elbows with the giants of journalism. We ate mousse and carefully cut sandwiches under a beautiful floral display. Life was grand. But then, the smell of tear gas started to enter the building. We couldn't help but think of the Titanic.

We had five minutes to leave the building or stay. There were no guarantees that we would ever be let in again. The ventilation system was turned off to prevent tear gas from entering. Funny how they intensified their tear-gassing just before Jean Chrétien's press conference.

While most left, we decided to stay. All journalists watched the action from our fourth story window. One journalist quipped, "These are the cheap seats." "Yeah, the nosebleeds," I replied, "Except the nosebleeds are going on down there."

Our window overlooked the oldest cemetery in Canada, right beside an old stone church on Rue St-Jean. The police gently walked over the graves and hid behind the church. As this was happening, three limousines with Canadian flags passed by. It was time for a little Q&A with Jean Chrétien. Everyone was allowed into the press conference this time.

They say that politics is theatre. The summit certainly was a drama with many characters and roles: anarchists, activists, cops, journalists, delegates and politicians. But what should be done with the main actor? Where should the scene be set? How about the International Press Theatre?

The International Press Theatre looked like a theatre: dark, stage-lit, long twelve-foot flags lit with many colours, exaggerated distances, a red carpet and a big gap between audience and actor. The journalists were asking Chrétien about democracy in Haiti, the protests outside, the "Democracy Clause," whether he felt slighted by not being asked to dine with George W. Bush first. A reporter from the *Economist* used the phrase "redistribution of wealth" in a question. Jean Chrétien told stories about the dinner he had just attended and how nice it was, how he's paid less than the "worst hockey player in the NHL"; but he didn't actually say anything of substance. Instead, he got irritated with the questions, cut off the question of the chief of the Assembly of First Nations, Matthew Coon Come, and cut the press conference short, saying that he had a meeting. How did he get away with that?

Just as soon as the press conference was over, we were allowed to leave the press building. We ran into Québec musicians who no longer wanted to play for the delegates and young kids who worked sixteen-hour days, getting paid minimum wage to empty garbage cans for the conference. They complained that no one at the summit cared if they lived or died. It seemed that the stench of tear gas was not the only bad odour left behind in Québec City.

From Behind the Barricades

Heather Majaury

I came to Québec City not sure on which side of the fence I would be. Last year I was denied a press pass to enter the Organization of American States (OAS) meeting in my own community of Windsor. Visions of similar bureaucratic run-arounds crept into my mind as I entered the accreditation office in Québec. A business sign outside of the office read "CIA" in big, bold letters. I nervously chuckled at the irony. The all too familiar whirr of helicopters, scanning the city from above, followed me as I once again waited to pick up my media accreditation. This haunting sound reminded me of the OAS meeting in Windsor, and I suddenly felt deeply connected to this city under siege.

Surprisingly, this time around, smiling faces greeted me at the accreditation office. It was quite a different atmosphere from the OAS meeting the year before, when I was escorted to a back room and told I could not record any conversations between myself and any OAS media organizers. I was informed that there wasn't enough space to include anyone from CJAM as invited press. Out of the over ninety passes awarded to other local media outlets, the OAS could not spare one more press pass for the local campus/community radio station.

This time I was ironically part of the two thousand plus international press core granted the privilege of covering the hemispheric elite as they staged their grand illusion cloaked as trade negotiations. Like the best of Broadway, this production emphasized style over substance. However, unlike any musical, the stars of this show would soon be waging chemical warfare against the very people they claimed to be representing. I thought about the dangers awaiting all those participating on the opposite side of the fence and compared it to my relative safety and comfort behind the barricade. This wall—erected to keep them out and me in—was ominous indeed.

It wasn't until I crossed to the other side of the wall that I confronted the true horror of social Darwinism packaged as "democracy." The entire downtown area of a major Canadian city lay behind barricades—emptied of nearly all its life, except for a very small number of aristocratic "representatives," their paid servants and the stoic men in blue who protect wasted space and uneasy silence. The only thing connecting me to the streets below was the whirring of the familiar helicopters.

On Day One of the summit, I learned a great deal about strict, systemic control of the press. We were all working from the same direct feeds, which were conveniently provided by an official broadcaster for the summit. Press conferences consisted of low-content photo opportunities and pre-rehearsed speeches. Press pool numbers were limited and there was absolutely no access to these conferences unless you were pre-approved by the summit organizers. Visions of Orwell's *1984* danced eerily in my mind.

It was on this day, with no prior notice, that the entire press centre behind the barricades was locked down for four hours in reaction to the infamous fence being pulled down at Boulevard René-Lévesque. We were reduced to watching the events on television. Some journalists played cards. Others ate. But mostly we waited, chatted, and I sang. While we were all waiting, pounding at the doors of the media centre grabbed our attention. It turned out the pounders were reporters who were stranded outside the building when the lock-down occurred. They were repeatedly tear gassed without protection and were not allowed to return inside for fear of contaminating the building. The sound of this pounding still sends shivers up my spine. I thought, "How can this charade of democracy continue to be upheld against such evidence to the contrary?"

But the charade continued. After getting tear gassed when I left the media centre on Friday night, I returned to the media detention centre on Day Two. This time we were given notice before lock-down. Reporters were given the choice to leave. Many did. After this, Jean Chrétien held an impromptu press conference. Quite tellingly, there were no longer enough reporters to fill the conference room. So this became my lucky day! I got to attend an actual press conference! I watched many reporters—who would never have gotten this chance under normal circumstances—ask the prime minister questions. Mr. Chrétien tried to shut them down whenever he could, but I believe this was a small, albeit hard-fought, victory for the free press. In the Orwellian reality of which I found myself a part in Québec, I was grateful for small mercies.

Although I must admit the food was excellent inside the perimeter, my impression of this newest media blockbuster entitled "The Summit of the Americas" was definitely thumbs down. Those of us in the ivory tower of international politics really did have the cheap seats when it came to the spectator sport of news gathering. Behind the glass of our viewers' booth, my escorts—the helicopters—made their transition from surveillance to tear-gas bombers. It was then that I realized I could no longer hear their familiar whirr. Inside the summit my connection to the heartbeat of the street was temporarily severed.

Standing on the fence of division: Through the eyes of a minority

Laura Burrows

i stand on a fiery line
i stand very close to division
i am part of three contrasting worlds
Jamaican, Italian and English
all in one, but i'm not one of all

i stood on a fence of division
it separated each by their class
i stood there enraged and felt my female black fury
and stayed focused on what was my mission

so my mission, to me, was quite clear
to abolish and destroy this state
i stood on the fence of division
my body a burden on the capitalist face

but what does this face really look like?
i knew it looked nothing like me
that made me even more furious
if it weren't for capitalism, what would racism be?

i stand on a line of division
every moment of every day
my fury did not end at the Summit
i make a call to my colourful people
INDISCREET, LOUD AND PROUD I SAY!

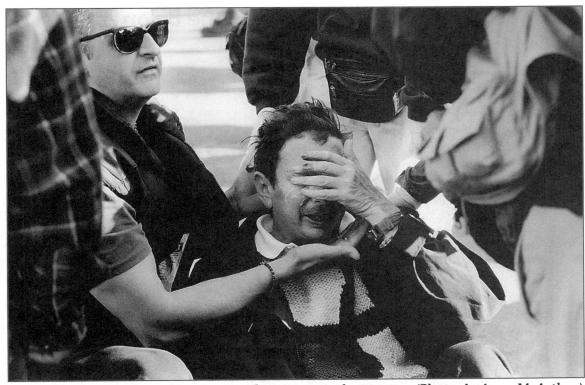

Medics administer first aid to a recently tear gassed protester. (Photo: Jo-Anne McArthur)

At the fence. GOMM action, Côte d'Abraham, Friday, April 26. (Photo: Erin George)

This Is Where Everyone Belongs
Greg Younger-Lewis

5 hands as fists
hit a steel drum
lying in the dirt
beside a trumpet glistenin'
gold, brap beating
seeking the ring of
the iron skeleton observatory
under the overpass

no one needs company
when the world is
the people's native dance

one sits in an acrylic orange sweater
no moments
no movements
still life
eyes closed, with circled
thumb and finger on her lotus
jean knees

she stretches, arrived
thru eternity, arms to the fore,
up to become a mime
from a grass knoll in the middle
and outside the universe,
under the overpass
of a highway in Québec City

this is where everyone belongs

ignorant of the ivory glowing
Jesus and the Royal Bank logo
watching from above,
everyone's hands clashing with

only the air between
the cobblestone bricks
and the grey-metal guard rail
of the off-ramp

thousands in a dirt-floor refuge
under the overpass
dustsmoke rising from
a 20-foot phoenix of burning fence flame
to competition in the sky, helicopters
swatting thick night,
irrelevant

this is where everyone belongs

rhythm clap and echo to the above
granite wall, on the edge of a cliff,
on Rue St-Paul
where the glints of government gas masks
stand in black
not moving as they did
to kick the last man
that fled from them, eye-grating gas, and
bombs,
the last one sealed with a leather-tooth club and boot

this is where everyone belongs
under the overpass at night
with the embrace of each other,
touching and not
touching, and dancing a-fly
loose hopping rave
tambourine metal dance
non-stop drum of
street signs

this is where everyone belongs
as one

Québec City: A Love Story

Emma Mirabella-Davis

Inside the medic building, I lay shivering in the blanket. Across from me is a kid who got hit in the neck with a rubber bullet. Spine damage. He is immobile, his checkered legs curled up against an invisible mamma, frozen in that state of pain and paralysis. The ambulance comes, large hospital workers shuffling into activist subterranean territory. A half-hour later I help one medic in the ally do detox from chemical exposure.

"Could you please take your outer layer off and put your shoes there?"

A tear-gas case with eyes running red stumbles into the gravel walkway. He holds his shoulders high, arms extended from his body with a look of shock and open-mouthed suffering. He's been hit in the stomach with a flaming canister so close that the chemicals have bonded to his clothes and skin. A chemical ice cream smear from the waist up. Shockingly, he has a cape on which only adds to my empathy, as if he went out there in good humor and met a harsh reprimand. We are unable to even stand next to him without our throats and eyes burning. He lifts his shirt to reveal a bloody mark on his abdomen where the canister struck, the flesh is burnt and cut. He looks at the amazing mother of the medic centre, Moe, with weeping eyes silently begging explanation.

"Moe's the kinda person who just takes your shit and …" a medic extrapolates with spiraling gestures, and it's true. As the kid in front of me with sagging long johns affirms, Moe is the saint of the medic block. Firm, serious and emotional, she supports the crew. Dealing with the shit. If you're ever tear gassed, find your way to Moe. She'll deal with you.

"It was really brutal out there. Really brutal."

I nod, tears running down my face. I have just entered the medic centre for the first time, separated from my group and shaking from the recent effect of the gas and concussion grenades. The shell shock of war reverberating in my ears. I'm a sensitive creature and putty in her arms.

"But I left them! I left my group! The canisters were exploding all around us! They were just firing and firing like they didn't care, like they were going to cut right through us!"

"One thing I'm serious about is that I don't want to hear anymore beating up of yourself. It was brutal out there. People are good at different things. Why do you think I work in here? No more beating up."

"Okay." I sniff.

"I'm really serious about that."

"Okay."

The medics are an amazing bunch—hearty, good communicators with spirits of gold. Radical med students in overalls, stethoscopes wagging around their necks as they rush from room to room. Sensitive punk rockers holding blasted activists' hands, repeating, "If there is anything you need, I'll be right here." Dumpster divers by day, healers by night. Ma, I'm going to be a medic. In the face of chemical exposure I don't do so hot it seems, but I'm really good at holding hands and flushing out people's eyes. I'll be there, supporting the troops on the frontlines with hugs and a water bottle. Ta da! Look for me!

The next day the police busted into the centre and forced Moe and her tribe of angels out into the tear gas at gunpoint. Even in war there are rules against attacking the medic centres. Not here. No place is a safe place here. Remember that.

At night my friends find me, jittery in my socks. I stand outside for a little and we hug and share the day's adventures. They had been tear gassed more times then they can count. The police are firing two kinds of gas now. The strong stuff and the really strong stuff. The really strong stuff comes out as a puff of mushroom from corporate guns. It's so toxic you're gasping like a fish and clawing your skin.

"BOOM! BOOM!" Up the streets we see the battles have moved to the thin walkways of the Old City like fires burning in the night. Concussion grenades explode a block away and flash-bangs hiss at their feet. The police have also attached flares to their tear-gas canisters, which explode in light and chemicals above your head.

A screech of tires on the other side of the crosswalk precedes two undercover cops as they jump out of a fish-belly-white van. They pin down this one kid, his head bent at an odd angle against the street.

Now in a supermarket along the way to the university where we are staying, I drift through the aisles like a ghost nobody believes in. The products around me seem impossibly violent and offensive in this atmosphere of war and moral famine.

"Puffy Marshmallows! Kids love 'em!"

"Tatertots!"

"Jelly beans are for Easter!"

"Buy one get one free!"

Frozen grape nuts. Nothing could terrify me more at this point as I glimpse existential symbolism in every candy-corn. This phantasmagoria of assembly-line, fun-lovin', finger-lickin' foodstuffs seems such a moot point. How could anyone who has been hit with tear gas or beaten or seen the shades and tides of this corporate incision and cruel horror infused with the normalization of evil ever eat … corn-nuts?

Throughout the aisles the others make jokes, and I find that I have nothing to say. Stunned into silence by something looming before me, dressed in riot gear, looking like G. Dubya, and stepping on the sensitivity of humanity.… The smell of tear gas is everywhere.

My lover and I attempt to talk about our separation on the street and end frustrated. The same thing had happened earlier.

The first time it happened was, well, the first time. We were too close. Near a tree. The cops in their inhuman gear, standing like juggernauts across the way, were just popping them like fireworks. Vengeful blasts of toxic waste. A burning ball of very hot chemical reactions happening in a metal can. It smelled like combustion. Explosion … then the gas. Of course we were too close. A canister blasted from a gun and angrily hovered above our heads, people shifting back and forth, pointing to where it was going to fall. "Right here! Right here!" The first chemical ghost grabbed us. Like a wall. Wham. That rag soaked in vinegar did nothing. All of a sudden I was in space without oxygen. I couldn't breathe at all, suffocating. We all stumbled down the stairs in between the buildings. Fuck, fuck, fuck! Eyes burning and chemicals clogging the tubes of my lungs. Then it was gone.

That was the worst thing about the gas. It got inside you. It became you. You breathed it in from your skin, your hair. It took away your smell. It was everywhere. In Philly and at other protests I could see the cops' faces. As long as they didn't get too close, you were fine. They could hit you, arrest you. But here, they were everywhere. Invisible.

Four of us. A meeting of the affinity group was called. They wanted to go back into the gas. I'd had enough. The blast of chemicals terrified me, and I felt my threshold had definitely been crossed. I do not excel in this area. Jordan, my lover, tried to calm me.

"Don't tell me to calm down. The tension between us is too great. I feel scapegoated because I don't wanna go back in there."

"We came here to do this kind of high-risk action. I want to go on."

I looked at her flaming green eyes.

"Maybe you did. You're a frontliner. I'm not. I do civil disobedience without chemicals— blocking traffic, street theatre media, theory and medic work. I don't excel on the frontlines, and I'm not supposed to. I'm sensitive to it. I'm a recounter, a storyteller."

"But we want to go back in. Are we going to split?"

I felt like the rat. The wimp. A position I had always been proud of. But now I was holding my lover and her two friends back. I decided to give it another shot.

"All right. Let's do it."

Back on the green, the canisters popped across the road. Each time we retreated down the steps, the chemicals would get closer. I did medic work and washed out people's faces. Finally a metallic clank hit the side wall and a canister landed in our safe space. The beast was moving in.

An overwhelming terror seized me as we hit the road up which the cops were advancing. I was numb with an animalistic fear deep in my throat. My instinct for survival kicked in as the dark troops with exploding poison and arms of metal advanced in riot gear. I saw red, death and the dread realization that they weren't holding anything back. This was a taste of war, and it was hell.

"Ohh … oh fuck … I wanna go. Let's get the fuck out of here!"

"You're just not calming down," Jordan sobbed, "I can't calm you down."

I assured her that I was all right. I just wanted to leave the red zone. As the explosions neared, it all seemed to be some horrible tapestry backdrop counterpointing my relationship issues with Jordan. All this shit was coming out in the streets of Québec, amid the tear gas and concussion grenades. We stood there yelling at each other in the noxious air and high-tension-wire streets of revolution, as our deepest issues surfaced like bubbles of smoke in water.

That's when the medic car cruised by like a chariot of rescue. We got the address and I got in. As the car started moving, she stumbled down the street alongside it. Jordan and I crushed each other's lips in kisses and repeatedly swore our love. I suddenly just wanted her to be safe from all this blasting.

"Come with me," I told her with tears in my eyes.

Misunderstanding my concern for her as need for myself, she wept back, "I'm not your caretaker, I love you." The car sped away like a top into the fray, as her form blurred and whipped behind me into the crowd like over-exposed video particles. My life was certainly taking a turn for the epic!

The university where we were staying is there, a thousand goblin forms wondering around the night. Weary after the first day we walk into the hall around the corner, down the steps and…

"Oh My God!" We are stunned into silence by the sight.

A 400-metre, indoor track field spreads out before us, and every single inch of it is filled with people sleeping, like an army of ants,. There must be eight thousand people here. Sleeping bags in every geometrical position, stretching out in a panorama of activists snuggling up on cold floors with each other or walking in and out.

"I had no idea there were so many of us!"

Before me is the multitude of the discontented, the passionate, the visionaries, the walkers, the frontrunners, the children of a lost time, the athletes of our decades, the nomads, the tribes, the loners, the artists, the makers, the doers. They are pirates of a decade in the wilderness, together, alone. Dry-mouthed and wide-eyed and rearranging and sleeping; their faces are all mine and on our faces we all have the same expression, but it is only in the morning that I realize what that look is. It is the look of innocence lost. Of a grim determination, of a sullen understanding that now this is a taste of war. A civil war. These fresh-faced kids with the jittery joy of doing mischief-as-protest, impassioned anti-corporate activists, had run smack into the dark waves of what human beings are capable of. The dark waves of fascism and the violent chemical stifling of dissent and freedom. Gone are their giddy looks of fun and papers about globalization. Gone are their student groups and graffiti and youthful exuberance. Now they have the look of weather-beaten statues. They could be from any time period; the lost tribes of Israel or street urchins, or people trapped in power struggles over land and freedom. But their hardness is not a hardness of hate or lack of emotion. It is of commitment. This is the real thing now. This is serious, this is real. We all are feeling in our bodies what we know to be true in our minds about the brutality of the takeover. This is our calling and our duty to do what we do best to stop them.

These kids are getting ready for a whole second day of tear gas, dreams and brutality.

My lover and I talk late into the night. She feels that she just knew she had to go on. I feel that she was not there for me when I needed her most. An affinity group should not force a member to stay in high-risk areas if she is freaking out. I feel deep shame at my inability to deal with the physical. She feels that I'm too sensitive and is offended by my characterization of her. I confess to having been jealous of David, a friend of hers in the group. She confesses to stifling me. As we talk, our fingers creep together and, through this strife, although still shaky on our feet, we are closer than ever before. I feel proud to be a wimp and to be sensitive to all this. That's my job. I tell her how proud I am of her ability to be a frontliner and get tear gassed and be so resistant. She has a quirky smile on her face as we nuzzle and she confesses that she loves me and can't explain it. Nothing is more romantic then sleeping on a cold, hard gymnasium floor, snuggling your sweetie at a protest in a room filled with eight thousand activists. I fall asleep with my breath on her eyelids.

Morning. We all agree to meet at the medic centre at sundown. We are all doing what we want to and feel comfortable with. We embrace and head out. No problem. Today is mostly legal. I'll do the legal march.

As the march commences, thousands strong, they shout through the bullhorn in English and French: "We are marching to René-Lévesque. Be careful. There are police along the way and they may try to stop us. They are armed and dangerous!"

Back in the place where we got tear gassed before, I'm faced with the beast. A huge ghost-head of tear gas and its thin, reaching tendrils drift from canisters exploding ahead of us. It occurs to me that, to the future tourists of Québec, this street will be a place to relax and picnic. To me it will always be a battleground, and I'll beam at some places and shudder at others, struck by the terror of that tree or this earth where the chemicals spilled from our eyes.

I nurse the waves coming back, as they sob or shake, faces red. I splash water off white stinging eyes and rub faces and hands with napkins.

"Ouvre les yeux. Ne touche pas. Ne touche pas."

As I sit six metres from the heat, eating my last peanut butter sandwich, I realize that the horror of war is exacerbated by the fact that, in the midst of it, human beings still stick to their behaviour. Like the subtlety of our lives, forced into brutality. I am reminded of a scene from "Jules and Jim" in which Jules remarks that war deprives humanity of the ability to fight their own personal battles. Yet it seems that, in the midst of the gas and actions, that's exactly what Jordan and I are doing.

By nightfall the cops have fired so much chemical gas that, from a distance the Old City looks like a cupcake with an ice-cream scoop of tear gas spilling over the wall and down into the New City. That's what hits you—the sheer amount of chemicals everywhere. It seems somehow fitting that corporate capitalism would use things toxic, synthetic, plastic and poisonous as their weapons of fear. The air is so stifling that night that you can't go six metres outside without a mask. We are holed up in a café run by supporters. Any attempt to leave sends us skipping back inside, woofing and shaking our heads like my dog did when she got skunked.

Down the highway ramp, below the café, a huge, impenetrable ice-cream slide of tear gas is headed right for us. The cops are moving down the highway into the New City like a marauding army of assassins, gassing anything in their path.

When the gas hits the café, the windows turn white with fog. Everyone groups together in the room. Suddenly the air starts smelling like tear gas and we realize that it is leaking inside.

A terrible claustrophobia grips the air. We may have to make a break for it. But there are only a handful of masks. People start taking off their shirts and stuffing them in the edges of the doors and windows to keep it airtight.

They have imposed a chemical curfew on a living city, without any thought of its effect on the citizens. The saddest thing for me is seeing a little old Québécois man—in gray tweeds, pork-pie hat and pleated pants, like those old-timers I love so much who sit on park benches—staggering through the poisonous air. He clutches his groceries, attempting to go home through the chemicals up to the Old City. I know he won't make it, just a few turns away the shit was red hot, and canisters are popping everywhere. Right near the medic centre. He is holding his embroidered handkerchief over his mouth and coughing and gasping for breath. We try to get him to come inside the café, or at least let us give him water, but he doesn't want it and goes on into the gas, confused and lost in a new violent age.

I see kids gassed, 12- and 13-year-olds, with smirks on their faces. I see a little puppy on a leash, passed out from the tear gas, its big eyes twitching, laying on its side in the street.

And just a few blocks away George W. Bush and his corporate controllers are talking about democracy. It makes you want to vomit but you're too dehydrated from tear gas. The worst part is that this hypocrisy is becoming commonplace. How tragic. How desperate for our world.

We're all alone here in this city at the ends of the earth. Where the cycloptic eye of the media has swivelled in its socket and left this city of space and time still and alone. It's a pocket in time, where the battle of the future rages.

I feel that through some horrible accident I misplaced my life before Québec. I see myself living blissfully unaware, as if I was looking back from death in longing. It is as if all that had vanished in the atomic bomb of corporate war. I cry for the old man on Rue d'Abraham. The future of our world. And for Jordan. So much for Jordan. I suddenly realize, like a resurrected creature, that to be alive is a wonderful thing. To be alive, to be in love and to live in peace is the most amazing thing in the history of this universe. And that is what we were fighting for in the tangled streets of Québec—for everyone to have the right to live in peace. To live full, free lives, free of poverty. Free of war.

"I'm doing the best I can!!!" I yell at no one in particular. And no one in particular answers.

"I'm doing the best I can!!!"

(Photo: Jo-Anne McArthur)

Photo Essay
Brian Burch

Tear gas fills the street
in my memory
and your photographs.

In my memory
police do not dress
like science fiction extras
but have faces, stretched into tragic masks.

Your pictures
show police in mirror-like visors,
dehumanized icons
facing banners
and peace sign-waving children.

Protesters confront tear gas fired by police after the wall of shame came
down. (Photo: Scott Harris)

Tear gas engulfs Rue St-Jean. (Photo: Jo-Anne McArthur)

voicing injustice

harassment and jail testimonies

In Québec, they used tear gas…

Heather Majaury

Slithering inside my skin,
This vapour,
Creeping into every organ.
Spinning in the shadows of this dark night
My world turns vertigo,
Skin twitching,
I am trembling.
Am I burning?
Help me!
I am falling….

She walks beside me.
Flatly she states…
"They're gonna poison the air, then sell it back to us,
Only those who can pay the price will survive…."
Visions hang heavy,
On the streets of this city under siege
In the shadow of this dark night
Skin twitching
I am trembling
Am I falling?
Help me!
I am burning….

A constant stream
I am crying
Grief, rage, loss….
Hope is a river flowing through me
Cleansing wounds carved with poison
These tears the women cry
For their lost children
Seep through the shadow of this dark night
What you do to my mother you do to me
All the women are weeping
And tear gas doth help us bleed.

Countless tear-gas canisters are launched into the crowds of people outside the perimeter near René Lévesque. (Photos: Vincent Pang)

Documenting Dissent
Ali Kazimi

Detained in Cornwall

I was just about to set up my tripod on Brookdale Street, in the heart of downtown Cornwall, Ontario, when car number six of the Cornwall Police pulled up beside me with its lights flashing. The officer stepped out and walked briskly towards me. He wanted to know who I was, what I was doing, could he see some identification. To say I was startled would be an understatement. I told him that I was an independent filmmaker and was about to take a shot of the street with my video camera. Why? Well, I was working on a film about someone who lived in Cornwall. Who was this person? Kim Fry I said. He took my driver's licence and examined it. Are you associated with the FTAA protests? I will be returning to Cornwall with Kim Fry and other York University students when they come for their teach-in this coming Wednesday. He was now visibly agitated. Would Kim Fry know about you if I asked her? Of course she would. Wait here while I run a check.

I waited as he got into his cruiser and called in my driver's licence, flipped out his notepad and wrote down my particulars. It was a bright, beautiful spring day, traffic was heavy and was getting heavier as people slowed down to take a good look at the puzzling sight of a South Asian filmmaker standing by the roadside with his camera and tripod next to a police cruiser with its lights flashing.

There has been a lot of writing about the criminalization of dissent, but documenting protesters also seems to be associated with illegal acts and is subject to suspicion in broad daylight. The officer knew about Kim Fry because she ran as a New Democratic Party candidate in Cornwall during the last federal election. She is now a graduate student at the Faculty of Environmental Studies at York and one of the organizers of the York University students going to Québec City.

A sergeant of the Cornwall Police had called Kim a couple of weeks earlier, after the local newspaper ran a story about the protesters coming to Cornwall from Toronto on their way to Québec City. According to Kim, he offered to act as a liaison between her and the city. He wanted to check in with her to ensure that there would be no violence and to make certain that she would not let her hometown down. Kim felt it was a polite and civil conversation that was intended to send a clear message.

I had met Kim's family, and there had been many discussions about how the police had been warning people about the threat of violence. Apparently, they had been advising people to shut down their businesses this coming Thursday. Kim and the York students were not the only ones coming to Cornwall. There was a border caravan of activists, which would start in Kingston and move to various U.S. border crossings to support American activists as they came across the border. Some protesters from Toronto were also expected to arrive to support the

Mohawks of the Akwesasne First Nation, whose land straddles the Canada–U.S. border at Cornwall. Some activists had stated that the Mohawks would exercise their right to sovereignty by keeping their border open if the U.S. and Canadian authorities shut the border down to U.S. activists.

There was no sign of violence in Cornwall but the police seemed to be on high alert; a South Asian man with a video camera and a tripod was enough to arouse suspicion and result in detainment.

I was documenting the journey of Kim Fry and her colleagues from York because I was struck by the questions of democratic rights raised by the security arrangements. The students' belief in their right to exercise their fundamental freedoms, which are enshrined in the *Charter of Rights*, is inspiring. Many had to confront their fears about police repression and the threat of violence. The three-metre security fence in Québec City and the threat of pepper spray, tear gas and rubber bullets from the six thousand police officers encircling Québec forced first-time and seasoned protesters alike to confront their fears.

I turned my camera towards the officer, who was sitting in his cruiser running a check on me, and pressed the start button. He waved to the camera and rolled down his window and asked if I was filming him. I said yes. Why? Because something like this has not happened to me in the fifteen years I have been making films. I asked him why I was being held. He said I should ask Kimberly Fry that question. His radio crackled. He asked me to step back and rolled up his window again. After several minutes he emerged from the car. His tone was conciliatory; he said, he hoped I understood that there had been all kinds of reports about violence being planned. It took them longer to check me out because their computers were slow today. They don't see media on the streets of Cornwall that often and, given the climate, he just had to check me out. I got my licence back. He wished me a good day and drove off.

I drove to Québec City that afternoon. The old citadel was getting ready to be besieged. Among the tourists and residents, the now notorious fence was still being erected. It was surreal to see traffic being held up in the narrow streets of Vieux Québec, as backhoes were used to move poles anchored in heavy concrete blocks. Tourists were enjoying the first warm day of the year, sitting on sidewalk cafés, looking at the Château Frontenac veiled by the three-metre fence glinting in the bright sunlight.

As I filmed a woman slowly and methodically tying a row of balloons along the fence, someone warned me that I was being photographed, and I turned to see a man scurrying away and glancing over his shoulder. This was the third time I had felt that I was being photographed, but this time I was certain. Graffiti sprayed on the concrete blocks of the fence proclaimed it to be the "Wall of Shame." The title became more apt as the summit approached. The Wall of Shame sent out its invisible extensions to the entire country when the Canadian Security and Intelligence Services declared protesters one of the greatest threats to national security; to Toronto, where heavily armed and belligerent police confronted a peaceful protest against the finance ministers' meeting last April; to Cornwall, where an independent filmmaker was detained for taking a shot of the main street.

Security breeds paranoia, which in turn breeds fear. You can rearrange the words in this equation but the impact is the same. Our democratic rights are slowly and steadily being eroded. This, we are told, is for our own safety and security. It all depends which side of the fence you are on.

Ambushed in Québec

It was a scene right out of a film about a repressive police state—except it happened in Canada, in Québec City.

On Sunday, April 22, after four physically and emotionally exhausting days in Cornwall and Québec City, a group of students from York University packed up their bags and got ready to leave the University of Laval. It was a gray wet day. The group had decided to take some food and supplies to the jail where the arrested protesters were being held. Two members had been released from jail the night before. In addition to the brutal beatings they got at the time of their arrest, they had been given poor food, had been kept in cramped cells and had been segregated according to race. The two were determined to return to the prison grounds to show solidarity with the protesters still inside. A few of their colleagues agreed to accompany them and they all set out, carrying boxes of organic food. Another group decided to go to the downtown core and help other protesters with the cleanup of the demonstration area. I had been filming these students from York for a couple of weeks and decided to accompany the group going to the prison.

As we stepped outside, it struck me as very odd that there was a helicopter hovering over the university grounds. I had watched helicopters being used as reconnaissance tools and command centres during the protests around the fence. The sound of helicopter rotors had become the norm; occasionally it became deafening as they hovered only a few metres above rooftops. We quickly learned to recognize that a hovering helicopter signified a hot spot in the protests.

The helicopter over the university seemed to be tracking us. I brushed this thought aside as the product of a tired and slightly paranoid mind. A few students coming from the bus stop warned us that police photographers in a van were documenting people ahead. I saw the van leave from a distance.

We bought bus tickets and were puzzled to see that there were no buses on campus. Someone called the transit authority and was told that they were not going to enter the campus for security reasons. A small protest march was going to walk down to the Québec Ministry of Justice, and it was assumed that this was the reason. While this was going on I photographed the CBC truck packing up their television gear and getting ready to leave. We walked outside the perimeter of the university to the main street. Some were trying to figure out in which direction to go. We crossed the wide street and stood on a small dividing island, on the other side of which ran a residential street. It had become quiet; the helicopter had drifted away.

Suddenly we heard sirens and squealing tires. We looked over our shoulders to see a convoy of four vans, three white and one blue, followed by two police cruisers. They seemed to be headed in our direction. When they suddenly split up, with one van taking the small residential street and three remaining on the main road, it struck us that they were coming for us. It all seemed to happen in slow motion. Within seconds we were surrounded.

The students had been warned a couple of days earlier that unmarked police vans were kidnapping people off the streets. Activist and writer Jaggi Singh had been kidnapped a couple of days earlier by undercover police using a similar van. I had seen several such vans on the streets in the city, but these were marked as Québec Provincial Police vehicles.

Twenty police officers dressed in green fatigues, five from each van, jumped out and rushed the students. I managed to pull my camera out of the camera bag and panned across the vans. As I swung around, I found myself isolated from the students who had rushed to form a defensive circle. The commanding officer, who looked and acted the part of a militia commander, saw me with the camera and came towards me. I kept calling out that I was an independent filmmaker.

I knew that the police had arrested photographers with press and security credentials. They had smashed the camera of at least one photographer and hit another in the chest with a rubber bullet. A Mexican journalist with summit accreditation languished in jail. Since we were to leave in a few hours, I was carrying all the tapes that I had shot over the past few days. I now ran the risk of losing all of them.

The commanding officer insisted that I put the camera in the bag immediately, otherwise I would be arrested. It was an aggressive, hostile order. I was asked for identification. Worried about my tapes and still in shock, I forgot to give him my membership card for the Canadian Independent Film Caucus. I doubt it would have made a difference. A business card came out of my wallet, and he grabbed it and mocked me for being a filmmaker. I was told to listen carefully. I was to leave the place immediately. I was to leave Québec. If I returned I would be arrested. Two other officers flanked me on either side. It was an illegal act, but taking a stand meant running the very real risk of losing all of my material. I had managed to shoot their arrival. I decided to walk down the block. I knew I was being watched by the police cars monitoring from a distance.

I later learned that the only Black student in the group had been the first to be pushed to the ground. His arms were twisted behind his back and he was the only one handcuffed. Another man had his arm twisted with a special hold and suffered from acute pain throughout the rest of the day. The students were prepared for an encounter with the police, and they refused to cooperate. They demanded to know if they were being arrested or detained and why. The police have their reasons, they were told. In contravention of the *Charter of Rights*, their belongings were searched, even when they repeatedly said that they did not consent to the search. Someone heard an officer say that they were angry about what had happened in the past few days. Kim Fry led a few students in singing, and they were told repeatedly to shut up.

They were told that the *Charter of Rights* did not matter because the *Riot Act* had been enforced. Even though the police refused to give their badge numbers, some students managed to write down a few badge numbers and the licence plates of the vans. Satisfied there was no threat from the students, the police ordered them to cross the street and then drove off at the same speed at which they had arrived.

I rejoined the group to find most of them badly shaken and shocked. Two police cars still kept watch from the corner of the street. Kim Fry gathered the group into a circle by the roadside; they sat down on the grass and sang to regain their composure. It was a small but remarkable act of defiance and strength.

It dawned on me that the helicopter had in fact been watching groups of people walking on the campus. The buses had been stopped so that people would be forced to leave the campus on foot; once outside, the police could easily ambush them.

What happened to us is what one would expect in a police state. Random acts of repression and intimidation against those who simply exercise their democratic rights to dissent are leading to a more radicalized youth to whom the state will respond with more repression, and the cycle will accelerate. Perhaps this is what they mean when they say that "free" trade will create a level playing field for all countries in the hemisphere. The repressive measures in many countries of the South, condoned and backed by the North, are coming home.

The message is clear: if you protest you will be treated like a political dissident in a police state. Enshrined as some rights might be in the Canadian Constitution, the *Charter of Rights* is only as strong as those who defend it. Politicians who congratulated the police for showing restraint and professionalism and declared that democracy was on the top of their agenda for the summit are not its defenders.

In spite of their rhetoric, the *Charter* is indeed a huge impediment to their agenda. They will chip away at it and justify cloaking it in tear gas in the name of national security. If this means terrorizing and intimidating the youth of the country who dare to stand up, so be it. If this means intimidating, harassing and silencing the media so that stories like these are not reported, so be it. By the way, if you happen to be a person of colour with a dissenting political view, you'd better watch out—you will be targeted.

Is this what democracy looks like?

Freedom at the fence. GOMM action, Côte d'Abraham, Friday, April 20. (Photo: Erin George)

A peaceful protester attempts to converse with the riot police. (Photo: Jo-Anne McArthur)

Québec police protect a shopping district well away from the perimeter. (Photo: Gian)

(Un)Reasonable Search and Seizure in Québec City: Lessons from an Emerging Filmmaker

Malcolm Rogge

I travelled to Québec on the weekend of the Summit of the Americas as a member of the Toronto Video Activist Collective and as part of a group of about fifteen independent Toronto filmmakers. I hadn't been in Québec City for even half an hour when I was roughly apprehended by a burly RCMP officer, searched, interrogated and treated like a suspected terrorist. My mistake was to arrive in Québec City at 2am and to pull out my video camera within the still unsecured perimeter area. The protests hadn't even started, and I had already come frighteningly close to being arrested. I learned some valuable lessons about the theory and practice of so-called "reasonable" search and seizure.

Looking at the map, I could tell that we were only two blocks from the infamous "Wall of Shame" surrounding the heart of the city. I started filming.

As our car rolled to a stop at the corner of Côte d'Abraham and Rue Dufferin, I caught my first glimpse of the fence.

"There it is! Do you see it?"

"That's it?! That's all it is?" the driver replied.

A row of concrete slabs topped with a chain link fence lined the side of the road. There were no police in sight. Cars were driving along like any other night. The perimeter area was still open to traffic.

We kept driving. As we turned onto Boulevard Réne-Lévesque, I saw a bright electronic sign: "Bienvenue au Sommet des Amériques!" I jumped out of the car, as any other documentary filmmaker would, and I began videotaping. It was a perfect shot for my film: "Welcome to the Summit of the Americas!"

As the brightly lit welcome sign switched from French to English and back again, two RCMP officers emerged from the shadows and walked quickly towards me. They shouted at me, asking me what I was filming. "Any reason that you're filming?"

They came right up to me. They were very fast. They began to fire questions at me, hardly giving me enough time to process one question before lobbing another my way. One of the officers pushed my camera down and told me to stop filming. I kept it rolling. The burly officer ordered me to show him what I'd been filming. It's not easy to keep your cool in highly tense encounters with the police, but somehow I managed to ask the right question at the right time:

"Am I doing anything illegal? Am I free to go?"

They told me that I was in a secure area.

"Oh, I didn't know that! I didn't see any sign or anything," I said, quite honestly. I told them we had just come around the corner and saw the electronic sign. I pointed to the sign and pronounced in my Anglo-français, *"Bienvenue au Sommet des Amériques."*

"Well take a hike," said the burly officer.

So I did. I started walking quickly towards the car, my heart racing in my throat. That was a very close call, I thought to myself. I learned my first lesson in political documentary filmmaking: if you're not corporate media, carrying a camera is like carrying a gun—you're automatically a suspect. Lesson two was also simple: don't expect the cops to put up signs telling you where you're not supposed to go.

As I got into the back seat of the car, I said to the driver, "Okay, let's get going." But before I could close the door, the burly officer came up from behind and held the car door open.

"Get out of the car!" he ordered.

Needless to say I was confused, having been just told by the same officer to "take a hike." Before I could say anything else, he grabbed me by my leather jacket and pulled me out of the car. Fuck! I thought to myself, I haven't even been in Québec City for half an hour and I'm going to be arrested.

He pushed me against the side of the car and took my video camera. He began to fumble with it. He looked into the viewfinder for a few seconds and then shouted out to the other officers, "He's been filming all of our secure sites." He repeated this point several times.

Moments before, I had been free to go; now suddenly I had become a suspected terrorist. I strenuously denied the accusations of filming secure sites. I told them that I had just filmed the outside of the fence as we drove around the corner.

The burly officer—whom I later learned was named Officer Fedor—ejected the videotape and confiscated it. By this time, about six frantic RCMP officers had surrounded the car.

Officers Fedor and Scott began to interrogate me aggressively. It was scary shit, so to speak. I had to make a quick decision about whether I should insist on my legal right to remain silent—and almost certainly be arrested—or whether I should answer their questions and hope they would eventually calm down. I had done nothing illegal, and I had no plans to engage in illegal activity. I had just arrived in Québec. The last thing I wanted was to spend the next twenty-four hours in a police station or five days in jail. I opted to answer their questions as truthfully as possible without compromising any other members of the group.

Officer Scott tried his very, very best to make me out to be a liar. I learned my third lesson: the cops will call you a liar over and over again; just ignore them, and don't let them get a rise out of you.

They demanded to know what I was really doing in Québec. They asked me why I was filming secure sites. When I insisted that I had only filmed the outside of the fence, Officer Scott asked me if I was calling them liars. I didn't answer that question. They took my wallet and searched it for my ID. They demanded to know to what organizations I belonged. That is absolutely none of your business, I thought. Legally speaking, I didn't have to answer any of their questions. But strategically, I thought it would help me if I told them that I was a member of the Liaison of Independent Filmmakers of Toronto. They checked out the licence plate of the car and asked me why we would rent a car and come all the way from Mississauga, Ontario. I repeated over and over again that I was an independent filmmaker and that I was here to film the demonstrations. They called me a liar. They called me an idiot. They told me I didn't act my age. They kept asking me, "What are you really doing here? Why were you filming all of our secure sites? Tell us the truth!"

They were relentless.

While I was being interrogated, a third RCMP officer took my backpack and searched every pocket meticulously. He emptied contents onto the back of the car. He examined my heavy battery pack. He found my filmmaking notebook and began to read it carefully. I explained that the notes were for film projects I had worked on a year earlier. One of those films was called "Scar(e)." He started reading very carefully. I learned my fourth lesson for documentary filmmakers: don't carry scripts for surrealist erotic films into potential danger zones that are crawling with cops who are trained to be paranoid.

Soon the Québec municipal police arrived. This was a lucky break. The Québec police officer actually listened to me as I tried my best to speak to him in broken French. He appeared to believe my story. He wasn't as paranoid as the rest of the gang. But he was a cop too, and he also searched me. He found my safety goggles in one pocket and found my bandanna soaked in lemon juice in a zip-top bag.

"Why do you have these goggles?" he asked.

"To protect my eyes in case of any emergency," I replied in broken French.

"But you already have glasses," he retorted.

"Exactly," I said. "I need to protect my eyes and my glasses or I won't be able to see anything."

He looked at the soaked bandanna.

"Citron." I said. *"C'est pour le gaz, s'il y a du gaz cette fin du semaine."*

He took my safety goggles and my lemon-soaked rag into his car. Meanwhile, the RCMP officers opened the trunk of the car. The burly Fedor frantically searched the entire contents of the trunk, presumably looking for anything that could be construed as a weapon or any evidence of a sinister plot against the summit. He found my computer in the back of the trunk.

"Why do you have a computer?" he asked. I told him that I used it to do my editing.

He pulled out one of my friend's bags and ordered me to open it.

"It's not my bag," I stated bluntly.

He pulled the straps apart, zipped the bag open and rifled through the clothes. Fedor stood upright, triumphant, when he found a gas mask and goggles buried among the clothes.

"So you're making a documentary, eh?" he asked sarcastically shaking the gas mask in front of my eyes. "Why would you need these if you were just making a documentary?"

Officer Fedor seized the eyewear and the gas mask, adding them to the collection of articles that he had already happily confiscated from me.

Then Officer Scott turned and shouted at me: "If you'd just told us in the first place that you were here to demonstrate, then we wouldn't have had to go through all of this. If you didn't lie to us about why you were here, we wouldn't have to had to do this. You can demonstrate if you want. There's nothing wrong with demonstrations. It's a free country. There are things that I'd like to demonstrate about too. But why did you tell us you were making a documentary, when you're really here to demonstrate?"

I told him that the two activities aren't mutually exclusive.

He actually stopped talking, for just a second.

Another officer started to rummage through my bag. He pulled out the copies of my zines. He held them under the streetlight and started reading them.

"Poetry," I told him.

It worked; after reading a couple of pages of my poetry, he put the zines back in my bag. Lucky for me, he didn't look through them all. One of my zines, called "Welcome to the Reagan Years: 2001," is dedicated to George Bush and his son George and is filled with diagrams and advertisements for guns and tanks taken from the *Canadian Military Journal*. If the RCMP had seen that zine, I'm quite sure they would have taken me to jail. I learned lesson number five: don't bring French situationist-inspired agitprop into red zones unless you're planning on explaining Dadaism to a bail-hearing officer.

Officer Fedor was a bit miffed that he didn't find anything incriminating in the trunk. He tried to slam the door shut and instead smashed the top of my lime green iMac. Fuck! I thought again.

"You damaged my computer," I said to Officer Fedor. He pushed the computer to the back of the trunk and slammed it shut. Then they searched the back seat of the car. One of the officers made me take out my Super-8 film camera and play it back for him.

"I can't," I told him, "It's film, it needs to be developed first."

"I think you're lying to me," he said, as he grabbed the camera and examined it. I showed him a box of unexposed film and explained to him that it was Kodak film, just like the film used in a normal film camera. I told him that I'd have to send it to the Kodak lab to be developed. He still didn't believe me and called one of his supervisors.

"He says that he can't play it back to me, but I don't believe him," the officer said to his supervisor. They looked at the camera and tried to figure out how it worked.

"What's on the film?" they asked again.

I told them the truth, "Beautiful construction sites in Toronto."

They gave me back my camera and I breathed a sigh of relief. They were beginning to lose their steam, and they had found absolutely nothing with which to incriminate me.

Eventually a very high-ranking RCMP officer arrived on the scene. The officers had a conference at the side of the road. Officers Fedor and Scott stood quietly on the sidewalk, away from me.

After enduring almost an hour and a half of interrogation and searches, I was approached by the big cheese RCMP officer. He gave me back my videotape and the rest of the items that his underlings had seized, including the page from my notebook about my film "Scar(e)."

"You seem like nice people," the supervisor said to me. "The area has not been secured yet, and you haven't been doing anything illegal," he continued. "But we are on full alert here though. It is a very tense situation, so please understand."

What he's saying is that he'll argue in court that it was a reasonable search, I thought to myself.

"Are we free to go?" I asked.

"Yes."

"Can I get the officers' badge numbers?"

"Yes."

I walked up to Officers Scott and Fedor and asked for their name and numbers. I went up to the window of the Québec City police car and asked for the car number and the constable's number. They were polite. There were no more insults. No more accusations. They played good cop. The interrogation was over, and now they were my friends. I wasn't a suspect anymore. Now we were "nice" people.

Maybe the shit would hit the fan now that the big cheese was there. Maybe they were embarrassed. Maybe they didn't care at all. Maybe it was just practice. Maybe it was just all in fun.... Maybe it was a reasonable interrogation.

I got back into the car, and we started off to the University of Laval. Just a block away we saw another car at the side of the road, surrounded by police officers. The trunk was open, and people were being searched. I learned lesson number five: this is only the beginning, we are all suspects now.

Riot police guard a breach in the infamous perimeter. (Photo: Gian)

Akwesasne Cross-Border Action, April 19, 2001: A Mohawk Community and OCAP Confront State Repression

Jeff Shantz

The Seaway International Bridge between Canada and the U.S. is situated on the lands of the Kanienkahaka Mohawk Nation at Akwesasne, a constant symbol of the imperialist powers' occupation of Native communities and a daily affront to Native self-determination. The international border, which the Seaway Bridge spans, divides the Mohawk community between rule by the Canadian state and rule by the U.S. Each day, that rule is asserted against the sovereignty of the Mohawk Nation as U.S. and Canadian authorities determine who crosses the border and who does not. Often that decision is made only after people have been subjected to such indignities as strip searches and interrogations.

Thursday, April 19, 2001, just a day before the main actions against the Free Trade Area of the Americas (FTAA) meetings in Québec City, an action was planned by Mohawks with support from the Ontario Coalition Against Poverty (OCAP), Anti-Racist Action (ARA), the Canadian Union of Public Employees (CUPE), the Canadian Union of Postal Workers (CUPW) and students from several high schools to open the border between Canada and the U.S. to allow U.S. activists to enter Canada on their way to Québec City. The action was intended to be an assertion of Mohawk sovereignty, an opportunity to expose the conditions in which Mohawks live and an act of solidarity with those travelling onward to fight against the brutality of corporate globalization. It built upon the long-standing relationship of mutual support between Mohawk warriors and OCAP.

It became clear immediately that state authorities would go to great lengths to prevent any solidarity between Mohawks, community groups and non-Mohawk activists intent upon challenging these conditions. The police presence was overwhelming as four to five hundred cops, including federal forces (Royal Canadian Mounted Police), provincial forces (Ontario Provincial Police) and municipal cops from the nearby city of Cornwall, descended on the community.

Several members of Toronto's Metro Intelligence—which keeps close tabs on every move OCAP makes—were on hand, including the head of Metro, Steve Irwin. They paid close attention to the caravan throughout the day, staying especially focused on those of us who eventually made it onto the bridge.

Counter-intelligence has been practised by state forces in Akwesasne and other Native communities for hundreds of years. It is part of the rule to which Native peoples have been subjected since colonization. However, in the weeks leading up to April 19, state forces stepped up procedures, organizing counter-intelligence campaigns and police disruptions at a high level.

It soon became clear that much time and money had been spent on massive campaigns of disinformation within the community at Akwesasne. Well-orchestrated radio and print campaigns warned residents that OCAP was bringing terrorists, sex offenders and murderers into the community. People were told to lock their doors and keep their children inside.

The action painfully revealed lingering splits within the community of Akwesasne. Band council, a conservative body with little credibility in the community (as opposed to the traditional tribal council), worked with the provincial police against protesters and organizers.

Band council held public meetings at which videos of the more dramatic confrontational footage from actions in Seattle, Washington D.C. and Philadelphia were shown. Residents were told that protesters were going to burn their homes and loot stores in a crazed rampage.

Later reports would reveal that fishers at Tyendinaga, who were catching walleye for the fish-fry feast to welcome activists, had been arrested in Mohawk waters on April 18, the day before the border action. As a result of these arrests, and of anti-Mohawk rallies planned for Belleville by non-Natives, many warriors chose to stay in Tyendinaga and deal with those potentially explosive situations.

When our caravan of about two hundred supporters first arrived in Akwesasne from the Canadian side, we were sent packing by provincial police, who told us we could not park anywhere near the bridge (even though we had parked away from the bridge). Not wanting to risk a confrontation before the action even got under way, we drove back into nearby Cornwall.

For several hours the caravan cooled its heels in a mall parking lot, wondering what was going to become of the day. We knew that a fish fry and feast had been planned on the U.S. side but it looked more and more like we would not have the opportunity to meet and exchange ideas, concerns and visions with those who were taking part in the gathering.

Finally, after great delay, Shawn Brant of Tyendinaga and an OCAP organizer arrived to meet with band council and police. After much discussion, an agreement was struck to allow our caravan onto the bridge to meet people crossing over from the U.S. side. The caravan agreed that the event would be peaceful and respectful of the community. We would simply meet folks coming from the southern side and welcome them across the border. Spirits lifted. We got the caravan in line and slowly set off for the bridge.

Our optimism was dashed almost as soon as the front of the caravan reached the bridge entrance. It seems we had been deceived. Police closed in on the caravan after the first three vehicles made it onto the bridge, stopping all remaining vehicles, including the buses, and turning everyone back to Cornwall. I was one of only eight people from our side who made it onto the bridge. Cops were lined up in the hundreds behind and on either side of us. We were forced to walk a gauntlet of police, lined one every three feet all the way out to the middle of the bridge, in what was clearly an act of intimidation.

From the Seaway we could see Mohawk residents in a fenced off area just alongside the bridge. The police had certainly gone to tremendous lengths to ensure as little direct engagement as possible between the people of Akwesasne and members of the caravan. It is, of course, long-standing colonialist practice to separate, divide and ultimately conquer. Eventually a couple of us made our way over and talked to folks through the fence while police photographed and videotaped us the entire time. The people told us that they were in support of people going to Québec City for the actions against the FTAA, but they were deeply concerned by the massive police presence in Akwesasne. Akwesasne, they said, was just now recovering from a ten-year period of intense police occupation, surveillance and violence inflicted on the community as a result of its militant support of the Mohawks of Kanewake and Ganasetake in their clash with the Canadian state at Oka. At that time state repression was such that the army stayed on Mohawk lands for two years. People feared increased repression and violence once again, and the presence of several hundred federal and provincial forces made them uneasy. It reminded them too much of the troubled times of a decade ago and no one wanted to risk reopening old wounds. The people wished us well, and as we returned to the bridge they gave us traditional words of solidarity.

The walk out to the middle of the bridge was somewhat surreal—though it was all too real: eight of us, including a month-old baby, walking along a gauntlet of several dozen grim, armed officers. In the background, behind the hundreds of police to the rear of us, was the spew and stench of the pulp plant, which regularly spits toxins into the air and water of Akwesasne.

Not sure what to expect next, we spotted in front of us at the arch of the bridge a boisterous, joyful and noisy procession waving banners and playing drums. Our fellow travellers had made it on from the south side. We smiled and hurried to greet them. They told us that the feast and gathering had gone relatively well, and they were anxious to meet up with people on the north shore.

At the entrance to Canada Customs and Immigration, Shawn Brant, an organizer with OCAP, spoke across the chain link fence to the community members gathered on the Akwesasne side of the fence. He spoke eloquently and forcefully against the efforts of the various state agents to keep us divided. He talked of the importance of learning from particular experiences of oppression and the necessity of making common cause. And he spoke of a new spirit of activism emerging in struggles against global capitalism (as in Québec City) and against the local agents of capitalism (as in OCAP's work in Ontario). The fences must come down and the borders must be opened. No more practices of divide and rule.

Of course, those practices were just what awaited activists at the Canadian border (despite all of the state's "Welcome" signs). People waited hours to get through Canada Customs and Immigration. Immigration and police stopped people from entering Canada and many were turned around. Independent reports suggest that about 100-150 people out of 350 on the bridge actually made it through customs. (The low numbers were partly a result of a solidarity action by some activists to turn around if even one person was denied entry.)

Those of us who did make it through to the U.S. were told, when later we wished to return to Canada, that we must walk the three kilometres back to Cornwall because our rides had already been turned back. When one of us, a mother with her newborn, argued that she could not make the walk, the police showed her no sympathy and yelled at her to keep walking, not allowing so much as a rest break. Thankfully, after much protest, some postal workers were permitted to pick them up and drive them to Cornwall, where the hundreds from the caravan and many locals cheered and waved a wonderful greeting.

Despite the tremendous difficulties, facing the action was an important beginning in renewed efforts to build alliances across the barriers that are deployed to keep oppressed communities from coming together, sharing experiences, strategies, resources and ideas and struggling together in solidarity. This is, after all, what states and capital fear most.

In addition to issues of state repression and sovereignty, warriors organized against the construction of and industrial dumping by toxic production plants in and around Akwesasne as well as the horrible experiences of poverty in the community. These are the features of the local face of corporate globalization and the reasons that permanent connections must be forged between Mohawks and anti-globalization movements in the region. And real connections were forged at Akwesasne, in addition to continued relations that have been built between warriors and OCAP. Indeed, Native communities have been at the forefront in organizing with OCAP a series of economic and political disruptions to take place in Ontario in the fall of 2001, with support actions in Québec, Detroit, Buffalo and beyond. These actions are being organized to make it impossible for the local agents of capital to impose their destructive economic and political agenda, which they arrogantly trumpet at international meetings such as those in Québec City.

For some, April 19, 2001 signalled the beginning of a new period. People stood up, despite the deep and present history of oppression, and faced the various levels of the state that continue to intrude upon their lives. Solidarity was forged against both the local and the global forces of repression and exploitation.

"Welcoming committee" at the Canada/U.S. border crossing at Akwesasne. (Photo: Gian)

The "gauntlet."
(Photo: Gian)

Not with a Whimper

Blair Anundson

big bosomed pop stars
pedalling ultra corporate images of coolness and sex appeal
for the sole purpose of selling soft drinks

thirty-second bursts of eye and ear candy
featuring steroid-toned men and anorexic women
designed to make you feel bad about yourself
so you'll buy the latest fragrance from Calvin Klein

news gives you the straight story
as long as it doesn't conflict with the corporate agenda

lives lived vicariously
through dramas, sitcoms, soaps

wanna be like mike

love, popularity and personal strength
now come in disposable containers

but don't dare challenge this
the greatest of empires
our ideas are holy and our intention just

"we are the hollow men"

we will Disney-fy the world
and lend it a helping Big Mac

"we are the stuffed men"

we will give you the dead things
in return for the live things

"our dried voices, when we whisper together"

we will give you a TV
in return for your culture

"are quiet and meaningless"

and if you should disagree
we have plenty of ways to deal with you

"the dead land"
gas, and spin
and the killers of men

"violent souls, but only as the hollow men, the stuffed men"

don't tell us of your wonderful dream
if it doesn't fit in with profit
it is no dream at all

"this is cactus land"

our capital, our possessions are dearer to

"the hollow men"
"the stuffed men"

are dearer to us than your

"headpiece filled with straw"

your measly dre—

"and voices are"

dreams
we will go on wi—

"and voices are"
rising

capital, democracy
can't you see, we'll give you democracy

"and voices are"
in the distance rising

democracy, see we're not so bad
we're...

"and voices are"
in the distance rising against the rule
of hollow images and their masters

we'll give you a VCR...

"and voices are"
in the distance rising against the tyrant
the dollar in all its forms
the tank and the rifle
the buyer and the seller
the consumer and the consumed
the master and the slave
are doomed to die

this is the way the world begins
this is the way the world begins
not with a whimper
but a shout

Activists take their protests into the night. (Photo: Jo-Anne Miller)

Imprisoned in Montréal

Alexis Robie

I was working on a production of a documentary that takes a closer look at the women and men who engage in protest in the U.S. To get the stories that the mainstream media misses, misrepresents or simply doesn't understand, I became involved with a few different groups of activists. One of these "collectives," which is a non-membership, non-ideological, consensus-based group, was planning to attend the FTAA protests in Québec. Since I had been "with them" since December 2000, I was also planning to go with them, camera in hand, to Québec.

In the months before the summit, mainstream media, government leaders, spokespeople and others had been trying to instill fear and paranoia among potential protesters and the community at large. I didn't understand how strong and effective these tactics were until the weekend of the protests.

On the morning of Tuesday, April 17, I joined fifty other people in New York City to take a bus to Burlington, Vermont, where people from all over the northeastern U.S. were mobilizing for a mass entry into Canada. People figured that it would be safer and more effective to get across the border as a large group.

For months there had been reports that some individuals were being told not to come to Canada for the protests. Others, like the ten New York City activists who were going to a spokescouncil meeting in Québec in January, were turned away at the border for no clear legal reason, other than the fact that they looked like stereotypical "protesters." Others were turned away because of their criminal records—crimes that were often nonviolent, symbolic, political actions in past demonstrations.

One of the main components of the proposed FTAA, which closely follows NAFTA's lead, is that corporations have the "right" to sue governments over legislation that impedes their profits. This agreement will also presumably include rights for capital and trade goods to cross borders without any "barriers." However, when it comes to people crossing those very same borders, the rules change so that anyone can be denied entry or held indefinitely.

Activists from the Mohawk community of Akwesasne, which straddles the Canada–U.S. border, had agreed to work with U.S. activists to help us gain entry into Canada via their border crossing, which is connected by two long bridges. The Mohawk people involved in the action had invited U.S. activists to a welcoming feast and fish fry. Our crossing was planned for April 19 around midday.

We began that morning at the Friends Centre in Burlington, Vermont, in thirty-five vehicles ranging from cars and station wagons to vans and buses. Colourful tinsel streamed from the vehicles as we took to the highway with an unwanted police escort. The caravan stretched nearly four kilometres, and a communication system of phones and walkie-talkies kept track of every vehicle and ensured a safe and successful journey.

We finally made it to the fish fry without incident and anarchists freely took off their masks as a sign of respect to the Mohawk people, who wanted to make this as peaceful and nonconfrontational as possible.

After plates of fried fish, dried venison, cornbread and pasta salad, we listened to speeches from members of the Mohawk community and indigenous leaders from other nations. Stacy Boots, a local Akwesasne organizer, spoke of the terrible conditions in their community and their desire for sovereignty over their traditional lands, including the border currently being controlled by U.S. and Canadian customs. He described the environmental disasters that continue to endanger not only their way of life but their very health; because of the ALCOA aluminum factory upstream, women on the reserve are encouraged *not* to breastfeed their children. Recent NAFTA legal disputes (for example, *Metalclad* vs. *Mexico, Ethyl* vs. *Canada, Methanex* vs. *California*) illustrate to how companies like ALCOA can sue governments for potential loss of profits if environmental legislation is enacted to limit their pollution output.

After the speakers, the demonstration began. All U.S. activists, except the drivers of the vehicles, went forward to the first bridge. A large march commenced with huge banners, drummers and even a stilt walker. People chanted and sang, and we all moved forward. We had agreed the night before that this would be an all-or-nothing action. Everyone gets in or nobody goes.

Because of the large mass of people on foot, things were a little hectic. Some people crossed, some were immediately turned away and others were kept for hours to be questioned about their "true" intentions in Canada. Luckily, I was allowed into Canada very quickly, with few questions.

I found myself walking alone, not knowing my next course of action. I saw a long line of people waiting to be questioned. I knew that I needed to get back to my affinity group, so I got a ride with a Mohawk police officer back into the U.S. The affinity group members decided that we should try again that night, together. None of us had criminal records and we were pretty clean-cut. We thought we had a very good chance, and we were actually pretty cocky about the whole thing.

That night, before we knew it, we came upon a small crossing in the woods. It was a two-lane road with a small building where the customs officers worked. It was about 11pm. The officers looked inside the van and asked us where we were from. What were we doing? Had we already tried to cross into Canada? Were we carrying any weapons of any sort? What did we do for a living? We answered all of the questions truthfully, but we were asked to pull over to the side. They asked us to step out of the car and eyed us suspiciously. They lobbed more questions our way. We were cordial, nervous and cracked stupid jokes to relax. For the next two hours we were forced to wait in the cold (it was below freezing) as they searched our bags and the van many times.

Finally the moment of truth came. We were asked into the office. There on the table was a gas mask. Almost immediately I remembered the bag I had neglected to search before coming to the border. It belonged to another videographer, who I was going to meet in Québec. She certainly wasn't a protester and had packed the mask only upon my suggestion. Oops. Big oops. But at least I had a good explanation, or so I thought.

The hostile customs officer glared at us and announced in a strangely proud tone that we were not allowed to enter Canada. Why? Because they had strong suspicion that we were up to no good; we would be a threat to Canada's national security. Why? Because of this gas mask and because of a video they found that they claimed was about civil disobedience. I explained again that I was an independent journalist and showed my Independent Media Centre press badge. I explained how in the course of covering protests professional journalists consider it actually very normal and appropriate, if not necessary, to carry a gas mask. I was doing it for my safety, so that I could get the best story. I told them that the video was in fact about groups of protesters involved in last year's demonstrations in Prague and the issues around the World Bank. The customs officers said I was a liar. They cut me off and did not let me finish my sentences. They said that I didn't need a gas mask and that I didn't need to be near the protest to tell the story of the protest (they jabbered on about super-powered telephoto lenses). I disagreed, but it didn't matter. The officers didn't care. They were not letting us in. So we got back in our van and we left. It was almost 3am.

The next day, Friday, April 20, five of us (three men and two women) regrouped and determined that we would try again. There was nothing wrong with what we were doing, and Canada had said that they would respect the right of people to protest. We would be honest. We searched everything again. The offending gas mask was thrown out, and we were ready to go.

Our van pulled up to a larger crossing on Highway 89 in Vermont at 10:30pm. We were told to come inside. Our bags were searched in front of us and, sure enough, they could find nothing. After they checked their computers again and again, the customs officers became aggressive. They said that we'd lied when we didn't volunteer the events of the night before immediately and that we were not cooperating. We said we'd answered all of their questions truthfully. They became argumentative, shouting and trying to provoke a reaction from us. We remained calm and answered their questions truthfully. They made us wait. My independent media status meant nothing to them. They didn't even want to see my press badge.

Hours later, the interrogations began. One by one we were taken into rooms to be questioned at length. I was officially detained at about 2:45am. A young-looking man with a chip on his shoulder questioned me. He asked me over and over what we were going to do, trying to put words in my mouth. He asked me if I was a member of a group that had been misrepresented in the media as either a terrorist or paramilitary group. He asked if I had been in Chiapas, México. He was pissed off.

I tried my best to defend myself and to gain his sympathy for this big "mistake." He seemed to soften up but detained me nonetheless. Around 3:30am, I was taken to a small white room, and for the first time in my life I was locked up. I was unable to do what I wanted. All I wanted to do at that point was give up.

At about 5:30am we were searched, handcuffed and put in a van with metal grates on the window and a glass divider keeping us from the driver's area. We left the border and drove towards Montréal.

We had made it into Canada. Of course this was not exactly the way I wanted to get there. The sun was beginning to come up and I was the only one in my small group that was awake. I couldn't believe this was happening—I was in handcuffs, heading towards some prison that was meant to hold me until the summit was over, at which point I would lose my status as a threat to the state and just become me again.

I was incredibly distressed but clung to an important consideration throughout the next fifty-odd hours: my situation was nothing compared to people who are forced into detention centres indefinitely because they are refugees or victims of (U.S.-sponsored?) terror campaigns or economic ruin. It was nothing compared to people whose justice is always in question because racism runs rampant on the streets and in the courts.

I was unhappy but I knew it would pass. I would be able to go back to my home, my cats, my love, my family. I would be able to find a job and not be haunted by the spectre of a criminal past. Who knows, I might even receive status points in activist circles by going through it, by being "hard core."

The detention centre was strange, surreal. I can offer only some visuals and moments. There were polite guards, who called us "sir" and then locked us in rooms, and semi-circles of guards moving with us wherever we went. There were enormous amounts of really good food and a rule against us mixing with the regular population, as it was explained that we were being treated better. (Why? Because we are not supposed to be here. So why are we? Shrugs.) There was playing soccer with pine cones, teaching each other chess and standing in the "courtyard" looking at fence after fence of barbed wire.

We eventually called legal supports in the U.S. and Canada and were given a free lawyer who met with all of us on his own dime. We were very angry. We were told that all of the charges were being dropped. (What were the charges anyway?) We could finally go home.

When tear gas and bullets weren't enough, police resorted to water cannons laced with pepper spray. (Photo: Steve Daniels)

(Photo: Karen Curtis)

You Could See the Shame on Their Faces

Liberty

So many little things stick out in my mind about what happened on the streets of Québec City. I'll never be able to forget the face of the riot cop who stepped out of formation to shoot a tear-gas canister, point blank, into the lap of a meditating man or the medic who held my hand as I walked in a daze through a cloud of tear gas. I'll never forget the couch that was set on fire and the ten-storey-high cloud of tear gas that rained down afterwards. I probably won't be allowed to forget the plastic bullet that hit me in the leg, nearly breaking it. I'll also never forget the camaraderie and love I felt from all those people out in the streets; as my friend Nicola described it, "I now trust punks dressed all in black more than I trust the cops." And I won't let myself forget the reason I was out there—to stop the FTAA; to stop exploitation of the earth, of indigenous peoples, of workers.

I was harassed the moment I stepped into Canada. I flew into Ottawa on my way to Québec, and I guess I was the first person immigration officials talked to about the summit, so they laid into me. "Why are you going to Québec? Why did you pack so light? Why do you have your driver's licence? Who paid for your ticket? Do you know the penalty for lying to an immigration officer? What are your parents' names? Do you have a criminal record? Are you lying to me?" They went through all my stuff, called all the phone numbers I had on me, photocopied my driver's licence and credit card and ran my name and my parents' names through their computer. They also gave me a visitor's visa that ran out in just over a week. I almost missed my plane to Québec.

Little did I realize that these immigration people were among the nicer government officials I was to meet, because on Saturday, April 21, at 6pm, I was arrested.

It started off so peacefully, about a hundred of us sitting in an alley (Côte Ste-Geneviève, I think) in front of a section of the fence that had been torn down. My friend Sokai and I were talking about leaving, seeing if anything exciting was happening at Côte d'Abraham. And then the police advanced. Sokai and I screamed at people to sit down and link arms but everybody ran. We just sat there with our arms linked. The RCMP shot off what they called smoke bombs, but I've never felt smoke that burned just like pepper spray. They yelled at us to move. We refused. They dragged us away from the gate. Sokai jumped on top of me in case they started beating us. I just screamed. They shocked him with a stun gun while he was still on top of me, and then they took him away.

One of the masked men told me I was under arrest. I refused to get up. He repeatedly shocked me with a stun gun, and another cop asked me if I wanted to get arrested. I told him I already was, so they handcuffed me and dragged me, one by the arm, the other by the collar of my shirt, back towards the broken fence. They dropped me on the curb and one knelt on me. I refused to give my name and, when I smiled at my friend, my arresting officer informed me that I wouldn't be smiling once I got to jail. He was finally right about something.

They put me on the blue police bus and, since I was the only woman they'd arrested, I was locked in a one-person cell surrounded by plexiglass and metal mesh. The men finally convinced the guards that I would be okay with the rest of them, so they let me sit in the back of the van. Six of us were arrested in the alley; one more man, who had gotten arrested further down the street, joined us a few hours later. Sokai had escaped his handcuffs, so he gave me back rubs and comforted me the whole time. We were on that bus for six hours.

They finally took us off the bus, one by one, starting with the men. They had to strip out in the cold, to get "decontaminated from the cayenne pepper ... I mean tear gas," as one guard informed us. I was afraid of what they would do to the women. Finally, I was escorted by two women in surgical masks, aprons and rubber gloves to a room just inside the building. They watched as I changed into the prison sweats, making me turn around, completely naked below the waist, though I had tried to retrieve some dignity by pulling the shirt down for cover. They insisted that I take off my necklace, something incredibly sacred to me. They wanted me to cut it off, but when I refused and pleaded with them they cut it off. Then I was taken to the showers and the medical centre. The medical woman asked me my name, and when I replied, "Liberty," she said, "That's not a name, that's a malady." I guess that says a lot about the mindset of the people in charge of our "justice."

Every time I turned around, they were trying to make me sign something, to tell my name. No one spoke English, or so they said, so they couldn't explain these forms I was to sign. They gave me the choice of a meat or cheese sandwich with milk. I'm vegan. They laughed when I suggested a peanut butter sandwich, so I went hungry. I was finally taken to the interrogation room, where I phoned my lawyer. He told me I had the right to unlimited calls to legal defence. Obviously, he didn't know that those running the prison, those who made the laws, didn't give a shit about those rights.

They finally took me to my cell, a one-person cell that already had two people in it; one more would come later that night. There were no sheets or pillows and only one mattress between us. The toilet sort of worked sometimes. In the middle of the night, three men stormed into the cell and shook us awake to read our tag numbers. Luckily, the women I was with were amazing, loving and funny, and we got along really well. We decorated our cell with toilet paper and maxi pad boxes, talked politics and sang songs.

I found out the next morning that Sokai was in the cell next to me. It was his birthday. For what seemed like hours, we held hands through the little windows in the doors of our cells. Throughout the day, people were taken for interrogation or fingerprinting. Sokai, who had also refused to give his name, got to call a lawyer and found out a lot of stuff—lawyers weren't being allowed in the jail because of the "riots." They told him we'd get vegan food if we gave our names.

Finally, after "dinner," they came for me, putting metal handcuffs around my already bruised wrists. I went, knowing that they were going to throw a lot of shit at me to get me to say my name. I went into the trailer, and the first words out of my mouth were "I want to call my lawyer." My interrogators and my guard laughed, but they did call the legal defence number. Once they left the room, I talked to a man who told me that the lawyers were in the jail, that I had every right to speak to them and that I should do everything I could to see them. So, I hung up and told my interrogators what I had heard and asked to see my lawyer.

They freaked out, throwing all these lies at me. "You don't have the right to see your lawyer. You're lucky you got to talk to him once. Someone is going to see if the lawyer is actually in the jail. Oh, we were going to let you see your lawyer in the visitors room, but now that you're being uncooperative, you have to go back to your cell." At one point, I grabbed the phone and started to call the legal defence number, but the interrogator ripped the phone away from me and threw it to the other side of the desk. That was it. I started chanting, "I want to see my lawyer." The interrogator replied, "Okay, you're going back to your cell." I told him that I wasn't going anywhere until I saw my lawyer. Two guards threw me to the floor, and six riot police came in, one with a video camera. They grabbed me by my wrists and ankles and carried me into this outdoor courtyard where all the trailers were. There must have been forty people in suits, wearing Summit of the Americas ID badges, just standing there, watching me be dragged, screaming and crying through the courtyard. As if the indignity wasn't enough, my sweat pants were falling down around my knees and I had no underwear because they had been taken when I was "decontaminated." I cried that I still had rights, that I still had some dignity, that I was in pain from them pulling my arms in different directions.

As they carried me into the cell block, everybody began yelling at them. They threw me in my cell, telling the women in there to turn around so they couldn't see what was going on. The riot police held me down, all six of them, until it was "safe" and the door had been closed. All I could do was cry; I wasn't much of a threat to them. Sokai said you could see the shame on their faces. I told everybody what happened, in the hope that anyone who got to talk to a lawyer could get the story to the outside world. The scariest thing was knowing that no one from the outside had any idea what was going on inside.

The prisoners in my cell block decided to chant, "We know our rights. We want to see our lawyers," until we got to see our lawyers. We chanted for forty-five minutes. The riot police came back in, removing people so that there was only one person left in each cell. Between the time they took the first few people and the time they came back for more, we had made a unanimous decision to hunger strike. Unfortunately, they took the rest of us. Sokai was left in his cell, and I was taken to the second floor.

This second night is mostly a blur. I talked for hours with my cell mate. She made me feel so empowered because she was so brave. She had been having an asthma attack in the middle of a cloud of tear gas when the cops ripped her mask off and arrested her. She was still sick but the guards just ignored her. She was moved by the middle of the night, along with the rest of the people in the cell block. I was left alone for hours. When they finally came to get me,

I just gave my name.

Within an hour and a half of giving my name, I was on the bus to leave the jail. It took most people hours and hours to get processed. They wanted me out of there badly. I never went in front of a judge. After they took my name, picture and fingerprints and gave me back my stuff, I wound up waiting in a holding cell with maybe twenty men in it, and one man in a wheelchair asked me my name. I told him and asked if Sokai was in there, and he was. We had a frantic five seconds of trying to figure out if both of us were okay before the guard pulled me away. As I exited the jail, the men in the cell cheered and chanted, "So-So-So, Solidarité!" I so regretted giving my name. Oh, and just before I left, they gave me peanut butter.

Before I could digest what was happening, I was on a bus headed to the middle of nowhere. I was dropped at a bus stop with no money and no idea where I was or where to go. Luckily, the jail support people outside Orsainville prison had followed us, and they took us back. Sokai remained in the jail, on hunger strike. So I waited for him,. He was finally released on $500 dollars bail after giving his name. He and I committed the exact same "crime," but our punishments were so different. It just shows how arbitrary this whole "justice" system is.

After being released from jail, I lost feeling in part of my right hand from being pulled around by my handcuffs. I had profound trouble sleeping and I found more bruises than I can count all over my body.

They did everything they could to make me forget I was human, to make me feel worthless, to make me turn my back on my principles. Though they tried to break us, we all have come out stronger, more militant and more dedicated to changing the world. When will they learn?

(Photo: Vincent Pang)

Several police assist with the arrest of a single activist. (Photo: Vincent Pang)

Liberated in Québec City

Angela Bischoff

"Honest Mom, I was just standing there on the street."

"Well you're lucky you're not here right now or I'd give you a lickin'."

She didn't get that I'd just spent the most radicalizing week of my life. Truly, I'd never felt so alive.

How could she have known through the corporate media filter what I'd witnessed with my own eyes for two days straight: thousands of peaceful protesters shot, beaten, jailed and gassed with poisons—including her beloved daughter—by her own "democratic" government.

I was standing alongside my bike on Boulevard Réne-Lévesque, blending into the crowd, as a wave of protesters came running for their lives. I stood stunned, like a deer caught in headlights, and before I could blink a throng of riot cops encircled us, batons swinging. Big monstrous testosterone-pumped, raging henchmen beat us to the ground, ripped off my gas mask and helmet, wrenched my chin in the process and bound my wrists behind my back with plastic ties.

I could hear my partner screaming out, demanding to be released, and I could see at least three cops sitting on top of him. As I sent a beam of love his way, proud of his defiance and meditating for his safety, my cop miraculously marched me over to stand alongside my man, to witness the assault. In the process we abandoned my bike and bag, which were promptly stolen.

I was then shoved behind the police line where the next round of cops awaited the command from above to attack. As I waited for my mug-shot to be taken, I watched the darkness close in on the peaceful protesters. The poison gas assault continued, luminescent in the night sky. The courage of the protesters buoyed my spirits, their seemingly infinite numbers swelling and receding with every onslaught. One young man walked right up to a cop near me and offered him a gift—it was refused. Others approached the riot cops standing at attention and tried to initiate conversation. Bebo (her jail name) shouted incessantly, "You do not have a right to detain me. I am being illegally arrested," while four robo-cops dressed in full riot regalia took pictures of each other with a little camera—to show their families, I suppose. I wondered if they were smiling for the camera behind their helmets and gas masks.

They kept us on the school bus all night long, hands tied behind our backs, no water, no food and no heat, freezing in our T-shirts. We weren't allowed to sit two to a seat. Women were at the back of the bus, men at the front. One francophone was mouthing off at a cop and was removed from us, never to be seen again. One anxious young woman had an asthma attack and was removed from the bus to be attended by medics.

We schemed some jail solidarity tactics, but only six others agreed to participate. Some blamed us for inciting the bad treatment from the cops. One cried out, "I'm not even an activist. I came with my boyfriend for a vacation."

At seven the next morning I was taken from the bus, stripped and "decontaminated" in the shower to wash the toxic gas from my skin. Dressed in gray prison sweats and slippers, I was escorted to my cell. Three of us middle-class women slept like sardines on the single, narrow cot as a homeless teen sat on the cold cement floor. The stale, white-flour, processed cheese sandwiches stacked up throughout the day as we all fasted, as much out of necessity as out of conviction. Instinctively we knew our bodies needed to detoxify from the poisons to which we had been subjected.

Until I was released without charge late that night, we chanted continuously "So-So-So, Solidarité," sang French nationalist songs, sang in harmony and banged rhythmically on the doors. The acoustics were mystical, reverberating throughout the cement cell block. We were all incensed. But we were also alive, and we wanted the world to hear us.

We shared our stories. I told of my horror when, near the epicentre of the battle, a middle-aged fellow ran towards me, stopping to flush out his gassed eyes with water. As he regained his sight, he suddenly collapsed beside me, his forehead gushing with blood. He had just been shot in the head. Miraculously, a medic appeared. As I gazed in horror towards the battlefront, I noticed my bike flag defiantly blowing in the haze—"Not For Sale" with a glorious earth emblazoned on it. That's when I noticed a hole right through the centre, just the size of the rubber bullet that had taken my comrade down.

While some jailbirds chattered and sang, others decorated their cells with orange rinds. Still others decorated their hair with threads from the mattress. Tony flooded his cell by overflowing his sink. His water protest worked—he got to see the human rights representative in the jail and was soon released.

Two guards came to my cell well after dark and said, "You are liberated." They gave me back my toxic clothes, escorted me to the highway and said, "You're free to go." I said, "Where shall I go?" They pointed down the highway, claiming there was a bus stop somewhere. I asked them for bus fare as my wallet had been abandoned by the police at the scene of the hostage taking, but they refused. Frozen, as my coat was also gone, and close to tears, I asked in desperation if there were any protesters. They directed me to the parking lot. As I approached the camp and realized I was among friends who cared about my welfare, I collapsed in a withering pile of sobs.

The Jail Solidarity Camp was to be my home for the next three days and nights as I awaited the release of my husband. Those three days healed my body and my soul; it was the closest to utopia I've ever been.

The camp spontaneously burst into existence on the second day of the police assaults. As busloads of political prisoners began flowing into the Orsainville prison, dozens gathered on the jail site to protest their brutal detention and to greet and support the hostages as they were released.

Volunteer legal support arrived. A stove appeared, along with chefs and a cornucopia of vegan food. Sleeping bags, sweaters, tents and tarps provided warmth. Radical cheerleaders and drums made it loud and clear to the prisoners inside that allies were outside awaiting their release.

The riot cops stood at attention, but the campers used the megaphone to tell them jokes. We imagined them giggling behind their shields and armour.

The camp had regular circle meetings with everyone present; these were translated into French and English. All decisions were made by consensus. We even wrote a press release by committee. Two security guards approached us and asked to speak with our leader. We offered them all of us or none. Thus began our collective negotiations with jail security, which continued daily until the shut down of the camp on the sixth day, after 456 of the 463 hostages had been released.

We built a bridge over the creek to a wooded area where the latrine was dug. We dug two compost pits near the kitchen tent; the cops were especially intrigued by this. The sleeping tarp protected more than thirty prostrate snorers from the wind and rain. The motor home housed the volunteer legal collective (paid for in part by the Green Party) and was used to charge batteries and cell phones.

Civil disobedience training sessions happened regularly after we were tipped off by a reporter that we would be raided. The raid never happened, but we were prepared with a get-away bicycle complete with quarters for the pay phone; a special warning alarm; a media liaison; and a plan of defence that included locking our arms and legs together in a circle.

On Monday morning, five busloads of political prisoners were released between 2am and 5am. Jail security had conveniently lost many inmates' clothing, boots and money. The air was close to freezing. Rather than giving the prisoners the option of being welcomed to our camp, prison employees whisked the prisoners out and abandoned them on the highway at a bus stop even though public transit wasn't running. We promptly sent cars to follow the buses, but jail security would give us wrong directions and tell our drivers that if they left they wouldn't be allowed back. Nevertheless, our drivers rescued a good many frozen and frightened souls as they tried to hitch hike that cold, dark morning.

That afternoon, while our lawyers held a press conference at the camp, another busload of released prisoners was whisked off. All the campers ran for the bus, waving and shouting at those inside to join the camp. A few media at the press conference rushed in to document the ruckus. The bus stopped briefly at the exit of the lot because of the heavy police presence. As the campers shouted, "Let them go, let them go," those on the bus repeated, "Let us go, let us go." In the heat of the moment, one of our campers dove in front of the bus and grabbed onto the chassis beneath. Four cops wrestled with his legs, two on either leg. The chanting continued, louder.

Sensing the chaos, the bus driver opened the door, freeing the hostages just as the four cops pried off the death-defying activist. This same guy had just that morning been released from jail and was wearing a bandanna to hide his identity. With cameras in tow, we all returned to the camp triumphant and free.

After my partner was released on bail we headed back to the city to try to reclaim our missing belongings. In the Old City of Québec, which just five days earlier had been a war zone, I could smell the tear gas in the air and see evidence of both the protesters (graffiti) and the fascist state (the fence). I felt jittery, defensive and emotional as I meandered through the streets, reliving the horror.

I made my way back to the University of Laval to reclaim our abandoned gear. Much of it had disappeared.

Disappointed and exhausted, I washed my face. My skin burned like fire from the remaining tear gas in the Québec City air. I sobbed as I remembered it all, the pain and the euphoria. My life had changed.

Tear gas was inescapable. (Photo: Emmie Tsumura)

(Photo: Vincent Pang)

Official observers assess the scene at Côte d'Abraham. (Photo: Steve Daniels)

Part Four

taking it home
part I:
reflections

Captivated by Conditions

Stephan Kim

Captivated by conditions of a system
expanding its enterprise while
depriving people of the freedom
most essential to the fabric of our being
and our attitude of apathy is rapidly
reducing our chance for change.

The people in positions of power,
though they've earned external
valour overcoming the others in war games,
have to sacrifice a part of their reflection,
so they cover hurt they share with those they beat

pretending not to see them on the street,
but who's to blame?
the basis of the pain is so ingrained
in the way we live our lives
it's even in the goods we buy.

Even over what we live and strive
for lies the darker side of our
monumental structures
erected directly in front of the sun
to underhandedly demand
we see the shadows they cast,
and nothing but their image,
an image of limitless progression,
while the concrete city covers the sky.

The nature inside of you and
I that unifies all life is steadily
getting embedded with edifices
that are deadening, letting
in nothing loving while
hovering over our shoulders,

Rage and Shine

Ladner Reet

When they grabbed me from the kitchen
And dragged me across the gravel
And cuffed me, my face
Face-down on the ground
I was not read my rights

When they locked me in a cage
for the whole Earth Day and Night
flicking lights on and off
in subtle psychological jerkings
I was not read my rights

Oú son mes droits et libertés?
Ask because rights are only ideas of what should happen.
Ideas which shatter with Authority attack-dog mentality
Thank you
You fuel the fire that roars against you

Gas Not Only Cause of Tears at Trade Summit

Anna Manzo

I had just taken a picture of José Bové, a French farmer who rose to international fame in 1999 for bulldozing a McDonald's under construction, when a tear-gas canister landed three metres away from us. We had been watching one of the dozens of street battles between demonstrators and police at the fence, which had been erected to protect the thirty-four heads of state who were in Québec City to negotiate the Free Trade Area of the Americas (FTAA) agreement, an attempt to extend the North American Free Trade Agreement (NAFTA) to the entire Western hemisphere. It was the first time I had been tear gassed, but it was not the first time that day that tears fell uncontrollably down my face.

A few hours before, Bové had spoken at the Peoples' Summit of the Americas, a conference of international labour, environmental, human rights and health care advocacy groups and policy experts who oppose the FTAA. Many of the individuals and organizational representatives at the Peoples' Summit discussed numerous economic alternatives to the neo-liberal model pushed by the U.S. When it was Bové's turn to address the summit, he explained how family farmers and peasants across all continents are the first victims of these "free trade" agreements. He further pointed out how these farmers are increasingly losing their land as a result of powerful countries like Canada and the U.S. "dumping" cheap crops into countries where subsistence farmers cannot compete.

Many of these farmers are fighting back. They are fighting so that countries can be sustained by their own agriculture, as they once were, and not be forced to depend on companies like Monsanto who wish only to sell farmers costly chemicals and, more recently, genetically modified seeds. These new and expensive seeds must be bought each season, unlike indigenous seeds that reproduce naturally over generations.

Resistance is growing around the world. In 1998, farmers and workers in India launched a "Monsanto Quit India" campaign on Quit India Day (August 9), the anniversary of Mahatma Gandhi's historic demand that the British leave India. Similarly, in Brazil, the Landless Workers' Movement (MST) recently formed to stop the spread of Monsanto soybeans and to uphold the state ban on genetically engineered crops in Rio Grande do Sul.

At the Peoples' Summit, indigenous rights activists spoke of their experiences in their native languages and, as their stories were translated into English, I was unexpectedly moved to tears, perhaps because they looked so much like the people in my parents' home country, the Philippines. I last visited the Philippines in 1998, during its centennial celebration of independence from Spanish rule. Victoria Tauli-Corpuz, who helped to coordinate the Declaration of Indigenous Women at the 1995 Beijing Women's Conference, and University of the Philippines professor Walden Bello told me how IMF structural adjustment programs and trade policies forced family farmers, who otherwise might have grown rice and other crops to feed their families, to compete with imports. They also explained how this precipitates widespread migration to impoverished areas of cities, as rural workers are pushed to look for low-paying, often dangerous work in urban areas, not unlike American farmers during the Industrial Revolution.

Tauli-Corpuz described how the biotechnology industry and the Human Genome Project were working on patenting the genetic material of indigenous communities around the world, including those of her tribe, the *Igorots,* without compensation or consent—a twenty-first-century example of neocolonialism and bio-piracy.

After visiting my Filipino relatives, I fully realized that two cultures collided in my ancestry. One, which was based on the principles of scarcity and "survival of the fittest," had circumnavigated the globe in an imperialistic quest for resources and peoples to exploit. The other culture was based more on sharing, cooperation and the sustainable use of resources, because nature was generally good to them. The Spanish conquistadors of my paternal ancestors' culture had superior weapons to conquer the tropical, indigenous peoples of my maternal ancestors' culture. These two peoples could not understand each others' experiences, needs and values because they could not speak each others' language. The cultural barriers were daunting and yet so similar to conflicts recurring in other lands throughout human history.

We now have the technology to communicate globally, transport goods overseas quickly and rid the world of its worst aspects of scarcity. But despite this, "first world" nations, with the help of multinational corporations, are still operating with an economic model based on the "exploitation of scarce resources." The model is not sustainable for the environment, nor for the human condition.

Many opponents of the FTAA say the agreement will widen income disparity by privatizing public institutions, such as education, health care, the prison system and utilities. Many critics also say the FTAA will extend the most controversial and extreme provisions of NAFTA to the entire hemisphere. They strongly oppose NAFTA's investor-protection provision, known as Chapter 11; this allows multinational corporations to sue democratically elected governments over labour, environmental, public health and safety laws that interfere with a corporation's profit-making ability. Canada, Mexico and the U.S. have all been sued under this NAFTA provision.

I need no artificially induced tears from tear gas to influence my opposition to unfair trade policies. I am especially touched and hopeful when I see and hear stories of thousands of students and workers around the world who are willing to endure arrests, tear gas and rubber bullets to fight for change. The image of students in Seattle raising their hands in peace signs nearly two years ago at the World Trade Organization demonstrations, and again in Québec City as they confronted rows of police in riot gear, will remain with me for a long time.

I sincerely hope the FTAA negotiators and other trade officials will someday stop the real tears of millions of people around the world whose suffering has been magnified unnecessarily by the greed of transnational corporations—the world's new conquistadors.

But perhaps the true sorrow and shame belong with the economically and politically powerful, who are pushing the world towards greater inequality and deprivation at a time when the technology and human enlightenment now exist to end the exploitation, wars and poverty that our ancestors have struggled to overcome for centuries.

The "Community Picnic" held in front of the Ministry of Agriculture drew a large crowd of protesters concerned about farm and food-safety issues, the dangers of GMOs and the impacts of life patents. (Photo: Leslie Menagh)

Analyzing Québec's Intifada

Scott Weinstein

I have been quite critical of our "anti-globalization movement" since the 1999 WTO protests in Seattle, and I was almost happy that the 2000 IMF/WB protests in Washington were somewhat of a tactical flop. My argument then was that it would force us to add more depth and diversity to our movement and forms of resistance, that protesting on the streets is a limited and superficial means of advancing our agenda.

To be frank, quite a few of us were very concerned that the direct action and street protests in Québec City would be a disaster. On a simple superficial tactical level, we realized that our numbers would be small, marginalized, uninspired and that the security plan would completely isolate and contain us. I was worried about the divisions in our movement and internal problems that were not being resolved constructively.

Washington was successful until the days of the protest, then it just petered out. The OAS protest in Windsor was somewhat of a bummer in that our numbers were small, unprepared and unenthusiastic. Afterwards, few people left feeling more confident about our effect–iveness. The G-20 events in Montréal were not too great either; the NGO conference received little publicity, and the street protesters got beat on by the police. Hardly three weeks before the events of Québec, SalAMI's Ottawa demo to release the FTAA texts was nice but lacked both energy and the large numbers expected. Good events continued to happen in South America, Europe, Asia, Africa and elsewhere but, since Seattle, North American events, with the exception of the U.S. Republican and Democratic conventions in 2000, seemed to be losing ground.

My hope going into the FTAA weekend was that any disaster would be limited to the Québec Left and that the rest of North America would escape the fallout. To the surprise of everyone, especially the organizers with whom I spoke, the weekend was much more positive and energizing than expected.

The FTAA protests started with the Peoples' Summit, which ended Friday. There was very good media coverage in Québec, and the event's final declaration slammed the FTAA for its purpose, content and clandestine process.

The union-organized march was huge, larger than the organizers expected. While it received little publicity, which we knew would happen, there is no doubt that the internal organizing that mobilized nearly sixty thousand people will further the broad-based opposition to corporate globalization.

The street protests dovetailed nicely into this framework of general public awareness and resistance. The sheer energy was inspiring not to just the younger protesters but to everyone. Taking down the security fence and challenging the robo-cops really resonated with lots of people in Canada who wouldn't dare engage in direct action out of personal fear. My concern that the more confrontational actions would scare away many was groundless. One nonviolent protester said, "It's not violent when you throw back the weapons of the state that they threw at you."

There was detailed analysis from the Peoples' Summit, widespread community and labour participation from the march and tremendous energy from the street. In the end, we maintained solidarity with each other, complemented each others' effects and appealed to a very broad-based spectrum of people. A new generation of activists and leadership is emerging, and these youth generally have an antiauthoritarian operating philosophy.

All of this advances the strategic objective, which is to build a broad-based resistance movement of global solidarity. I still think we are halfway through the beginning stages of developing the movement. We haven't yet developed effective structural coherence with each other, nor is there a common vision of what type of world we are fighting for. But two years ago we didn't experience anything that felt like a movement. As frightening as our times are now, there are objective reasons to feel optimistic.

We already had achieved a major victory before stepping into Québec City. Conscious-ness-raising is vital to resistance. The key organizations calling for the FTAA actions (CASA, CLAC, GOMM and the OQP2001) concentrated on political education and, for the most part, put training and tactical planning on the back burner. The movement has exploded because of the activities and also the controversies that we generate. Sometimes simply "fucking shit up" is better than doing nothing, as heat generates attention. No matter how much the media may try to focus on us instead of the issue of corporate globalization, awareness is always being raised about the issue.

To be sure, all of the contradictions and internal deficiencies in the Québec Left remain. However, we all understand that the immeasurable psychological energy we get from a positive action boosts our ability to go forward and recommit to the hard work ahead. The divisions over tactics and the sectarianism, which was a major problem among organizations in Montréal but less so in Québec City, appear to be closing as a result of the positive energy we felt at the Québec protests. This can only help the broad movement overall.

My position has always been that the movement to establish global solidarity and oppose corporate globalism must be broad-based with diverse methods of engagement and great depth. No one method of engagement, be it street protests, NGO work or community organizing, can succeed by itself.

Our challenge always has been to be as inclusive as possible. We must recognize that a diversity of communities, using a diversity of approaches, is much more powerful than monocultures and monotactics. For example, the state learned quickly how to counter the Direct Action Network's direct action blueprint after Seattle and thus has been able to guarantee security at subsequent summits. However, they are not able also to counter groups of senior citizens demanding public health care protection, NGOs releasing critical analysis reports on the effects of NAFTA on domestic wages, Thai activists linking their AIDS epidemic to the results of neo-liberal policies that have increased the sex trade industry in their country, and union activists withdrawing from the two-party electoral system. Nor are the ruling elites able to counter the visceral opposition in the streets, no matter what the actual tactical objective is. Beyond that, what is our common vision for a new world? What does "social solidarity" and "direct democracy" look like in everyday life, when we are not protesting?

Last, the success of the Québec protests was largely due to the engagement of the local population in a major protest. The public opposition to the FTAA summit and the security measures had been evident and public for months. The neighbourhood of St-Jean Baptiste, which the security fence invaded, had been well organized with a functioning community council and a solid working relationship among merchants, residents and anti-FTAA organizers. In the end, it was not the organized Left holding the streets but the local residents, who established a brief period of popular insurrectionary power. However, there is a quantitative and qualitative leap from discontent to active solidarity and opposition.

In conclusion, the three major activities in Québec—the Peoples' Summit, the street protests and the union march—were successful. They were well-supported, brave and very well-attended. They had coherence. Their message and demands against corporate globalization had generally complementary, if not similar, positions about corporate globalization, even though there are still major gaps about our position on capitalism. We enjoyed general solidarity with each other and an absence of the bitterness that followed Seattle. Most are leaving with enthusiasm to carry on struggle.

Québec was a revitalizing experience for the movement. That's a tremendous victory!

Delegates at the Agricultural Forum of the People's Summit share experiences and concerns. (Photo: Leslie Menagh)

Large crowds participate in Saturday's march. (Photo: Jo-Anne McArthur)

On a march from Laval to the perimeter. (Photo: Jo-Anne McArthur)

Québec — Je me souviens

François Pelletier

I woke up the morning after the summit, asking myself what's left. Tens of thousands of people visited us and protested and then disappeared. Countless journalists came to see blood gush and gas thrown, and they also returned home to once again talk about the heroic exploits of Céline Dion. Many police officers, helmeted, masked, armed, paid, frustrated and brainwashed, came to pollute our air; later, they returned home to attend to shoplifters and street gangs and perpetuate the cycle of oppression.

But now, I ask myself what will citizens remember about the Québec protests. Will it be that police brutality actually exists or that the trouble-making protesters should have stayed home instead of attacking their old and beautiful city? I think what will stay in the minds of most is the bitter taste of gas and vinegar. More importantly, I must point out that it is unfortunate that almost everybody here in Québec forgot the real reason for the coming of such a plethora of people to our fair city: the much-disputed FTAA! In fact, thousands of people arrived to voice their dissatisfaction *vis-à-vis* the latest inter-American trade manoeuvres, but the issue of police brutality quickly became the only reason they were here in Québec City.

This oversight ended up costing protesters, for it appeared that the media—the alternative press as much as the mainstream press—also erased concerns about the FTAA from their radar screens, which I tend to believe is intentional. They wanted shocking images and sound bites, whatever would "sell"; and the worst thing is that we gave them more than they could handle. They inaccurately used terms such as "anarchy" and "guerrilla" to further their own agendas. They were satisfied to portray the Black Bloc as a bunch of tourists who were in the city for nothing more than the pure pleasure of rioting. This so-called Black Bloc came for the same reasons as everyone else, but unfortunately they also forgot why they were here.

Maybe we need to reflect. In fact, let's ask ourselves why groups of protesters forgot the "Fuck you, go away, FTAA" and replaced it with "Break down the wall, break down the wall!"

Like you, I forgot, most likely sooner rather than later, what was at stake, what was being discussed behind clouds of poisonous gas. The proof is that I was part of the frustrated mob that only wanted the fucking wall to come down. I had the same convictions and was guilty of the same oversights as the people dressed in black who the media unsparingly portrayed as the root of all evil. I might not have had those particular convictions when I arrived in the city but, please, place some of the blame squarely on my shoulders instead of always blaming "them." We were all in the same boat together and we all readily pushed aside the most important issues. Don't forget that!

When people tell me that Québec 2001 will soon be forgotten, I will dutifully respond: Québec—*Je me souviens!*

The Media Army

Max Spencer and Nox

Provocation and Intimidation

Without a doubt, before the Summit of the Americas even began, the erection of the security perimeter constituted an unacceptable obstacle to the fundamental rights of expression and protest guaranteed under the *Charter of Rights and Freedoms*. Moreover, in all the forms it assumed during the summit, it remained much more than a direct challenge to the rights of dissent. The infamous "Wall of Shame" turned out not only to be the stronghold around which police strategy revolved but, more importantly, in the eyes of the media it became an unquestionable feature of the summit, something that was not an issue in and of itself.

And so it was that public relations, a subtler weapon than a truncheon or nightstick, took on an equally crucial role during the summit. This began long before the summit, in a brilliantly orchestrated campaign of intimidation and provocation. Among the thousands of articles and reports released in the weeks, or even months, preceding the summit were such sensational details as the following: "Summit of the Americas: The RCMP is not fooling around with security"; "At least six thousand police will be working during the summit—instead of the five thousand previously estimated. This extra backup confirms that authorities are expecting the worst possible scenario"; "The provincial police are preparing for war."

This public relations campaign was organized and carried out by federal government strategists and the numerous police forces involved in summit security. It was a campaign of intimidation, aimed at discouraging potential protesters from making the trip to Québec and frightening others altogether. Even our prime minister went so far as to insult the protesters, and he attempted to minimize their impact on summit deliberations, saying, "They won't stop me from sleeping."

Action

The police strategy used in Québec reminds us of the new military strategies first used by the "allies" in Iraq and by NATO in Kosovo—surgical strikes, long-distance confrontations, kidnapping of supposed leaders, very little hand-to-hand combat. The objective is twofold: limit the number of police injuries and limit the media's ability to condemn acts of police violence. To justify their actions, the powers-that-be put all protesters, peaceful and not-so-peaceful, in the same boat. That this intentional lack of judgement on the part of the police played a major role in the outcome and the number of direct actions and so-called "violent" acts is unquestionable.

The original security perimeter soon found itself surrounded by a second perimeter—this one more noxious, a perimeter of poisonous gas and water cannons—within which passersby and protesters alike risked being assaulted at every instant. How many peaceful protesters played the role of a human target? How many were gassed or pepper sprayed, their only crime being near the fence? How many of those peaceful protesters, targeted by the police, decided to retaliate against the provocative attacks? Who could possibly blame them?

From a public relations perspective, firing rubber bullets mostly goes unnoticed and is difficult to photograph, and gassing protesters goes over better than beating protesters.

In the Place des Amériques, an area on René-Lévesque occupied permanently by television crews, police oppression was kept to a minimum, perhaps even cautiously avoided. However, in the small streets and alleyways of the St-Jean Baptiste neighbourhood, where bullets were fired indiscriminately, where apartments were gassed without reason, where cameras were few and far between, the security forces showed their true colours. They were able to somehow justify their actions in this tiny, unprotected neighbourhood by pointing to what was happening in the lower city, several kilometres away, where there were cameras watching and where they dared not go.

Police violence begins when the authorities show weakness. Consequently, the violence we saw on the part of the security forces during the weekend of the summit was the logical consequence of an illegitimate security perimeter and the closed-door meeting that was taking place behind it. Just like in all dictatorships and totalitarian states, power, because it is illegitimate, is maintained by an oppressive and violent police state.

After the summit, the public relations strategy realized its finest hour; all we read and heard about in the media was the government's satisfaction with the police. For those of us who had the opportunity to witness and take part in the Québec scene, it was evident that the media failed to fulfil their role and demonstrated their natural inclination towards the establishment, of which they are all-too-obvious members. "Québec established new standards in terms of security," claimed Québec Minister of Public Security, Serge Menard. The press soaked up every word he said.

Obviously, this was not someone who was at l'Ilôt Fleuri late Saturday night and early Sunday morning, when random acts of police brutality—brutal police shootings, the violent kidnapping of unarmed and peaceful protesters and the summary arrest of over two hundred people—remained conveniently undocumented by the media.

Scapegoating and the Black Bloc

Reading any newspaper in Québec could easily lead one to believe that all or nearly all of the protesters were members of the ominous Back Bloc. Journalists and other media representatives fell into the police's public relations trap aimed at turning public opinion against protest actions. They played the game to perfection, even going so far as to brand the protesters as "insignificant punks," "little rich kids with full stomachs," "excitable young ones who just recently found out what 'democracy' means, owing to a surprise dictionary visit"—a litany of insults attempting to undermine dissent.

The public relations strategy counted on the media to project any blame arising from the protests onto out-of-town scapegoats (read Black Bloc) before the fact. The media ended their campaign here, never delving into who these potential troublemakers were or what the true likelihood of the utter destruction of their city was. Of course, through it all, there was no mention of what the Black Bloc actually stood for; in fact, part of the strategy was to encourage the farcical notion that they believe in nothing—total anarchy.

What Didn't Happen

I could go on and on about the many creative and inspiring events at this large convergence. The festive atmosphere and the nonviolent radicals, who were engaged in sit-ins and human chains and repeatedly gassed regardless of their proximity (or lack thereof) to the perimeter, were truly inspiring. It was the members of the Deconstructionist Institute for Surreal Topology (not activist Jaggi Singh) who had the brilliant idea of constructing a giant catapult to launch cutesy teddy bears, who conveniently were immune to the tear gas and tagged with protest slogans, over the perimeter towards the police line. The protesters were hardly all "violent."

Nevertheless, because the teddy bears and massive nonviolent contingent ran in direct opposition to the government's and police services' discourse, TV coverage excluded these images, focusing only on "violent" encounters. It was a public relations coup.

However, what was missing in the "news" was exactly what was striking about the protests in Québec—the impressive meeting of knowledgeable and articulate people from different corners of the globe, who are overtly aware of the negative effects of capital on people and the environment. But in the media's strategy, this meeting became synonymous with violence before and especially during the Summit of the Americas.

Of course, this isn't anything new. We've known for a long time that the media aids and abets those in power, acting as accomplices in their projects. What seems new to me is that without the media's knowledge (?), the powerful in society have begun to use them more like a weapon, allowing them to prepare their actions, launch their assaults and gain acceptance for their brutal interventions.

Counterspin

Anne Marie Wierzbicki

creative passions blazed
it was a
two hour
two night
debatefest

audience members
anxiously awaited their chance to speak
then erupted into Avi's mic
from the bottom of their beings

he tweaked the heel of the monster
as it flogged its sole organizing option
"free" trade

spoke its one speak
money speak
which practices the might of
tear gas
rubber bullets
water cannon
concussion bombs
exclusion

the top 30 economies of the world
measured by gnp, gdp
some false rule of product
include Exxon, DaimlerChrysler, Shell

thus gas and cars and cars and gas
outrank 90% of Latin American countries
and all the countries of Africa but South Africa
which do not make the top 100

insurance companies do and

Walmart is higher than
Exxon DaimlerChrysler Shell

which countries,
would you say,
are up with them
is yours in the list
these ruling corporate economies
their power is might and
we must be like mites upon them
our voices blanketing the streets
that surround them
crossing the airwaves
and the networks
drumming the chants of the tribes

Rue St-Jean. (Photo: Jo-Anne McArthur)

(Photo: Jen Chang)

Free Media and Free Trade: Redefining the Vernacular

T.M. Abdelazim

The Agreements

Highlights of Agreements at the Thirty-Four-Nation Summit of the Americas in Québec:

- Open their markets by December 2005
- Exclude undemocratic nations from free trade
- Combat poverty and inequality
- Improve access to quality education
- Promote internationally recognized labour standards
- Ensure safe and healthy work conditions for migrants
- Respect human rights and fundamental freedoms
- Combat global drug problem and related crimes
- Combat AIDS and its consequences
- Take steps to protect the environment and pursue renewable energy initiatives
- Share knowledge to spread the technology revolution

I found this in my local paper on Monday, April 23, 2001. This is how the Associated Press (AP) neatly summed up the package deal authored and signed by the thirty-four member states in Québec City. The Saturday spray of tear gas that I had endured during the protest had abated, but the sight of this housekeeping list made me squint in disbelief. The thought of post-traumatic, chemical-induced hallucination wormed through my thought process: *Am I really reading this shit correctly?*

This fiction should win the year's Booker Prize. Throw in a Pushcart as well. The media's absurdly thin critique of the Free Trade Area of the Americas agreement only deepens the suspicion that its mantra of being a "free press" is just as onerous as the Americas' concept of "free trade."

Since the FTAA seeks to expand the framework of the North American Free Trade Agreement to all of the Americas, a logical precursor to such a move would be a thorough review of NAFTA's benefits. Is that model something to emulate and expand? Has it worked? The media neglected this simple and logical prologue. Strangely absent was any review of what was soon to be a major overhaul of American and Caribbean economic and trade alliances. The secrecy with which the FTAA was handled—from its initiation to the very meetings themselves—should intimate its less than democratic concerns.

In an effort to fill this media gap, I will challenge the candied, itemized sound bites offered to us by the AP and the mainstream media in general. The systematic deficiencies of NAFTA and free trade reveal themselves too readily, which might explain why the media outlets—tools to manufacture consent for pro-business operatives—unanimously ignored such a review. But before I focus on some of the "highlights" of the agreement, I'd like to first briefly reflect on my experience at the protest in Québec City.

Would nearly a hundred thousand people convene in numerous satellite cities as well as Québec if the "highlights" were accurate? No, of course not. The issue, of course, is one of information or, rather, *disinformation*.

For instance, was the use of tear gas warranted? Did you know that tear gas was fired in the face of hundreds of protesters practising civil disobedience? I watched it happen. Two blocks removed from the focal point of the clashes, I watched hundreds of sit-down protesters panic and race down three levels of steep aluminum steps or jump over a highway wall to scale down forty feet of dangerous rock face to escape it. I spoke to a few of them up-close—their faces were swollen, blood red and blistered.

Consider this: the campaign of power is won and lost with words. Democratic citizens— operating within the code of civil disobedience, fenced off by a five-kilometre buffer zone from a consortium of national leaders discussing behind closed doors the transition to so-called "transparent" economies and borders—are blasted in the face with tear gas, and it's called "crowd control."

Approach the pundits of free market trade as linguistic salespeople offering you a vernacular. You can choose to accept or refuse it, seek salvation within its code or shun and repeal it on moral grounds, but always approach it with the understanding that it is a perfectly engineered word campaign to further a design. The question is: Do you want to be part of that design?

Exclude Undemocratic Nations from Trade

This was written solely for Venezuela and Peru. Hugo Chavez and Miguel Toledo (the apparent successor to Fujimoro) are the respective leaders of these two nations who have shown socialistic tendencies. Thomas Friedman, a *New York Times* columnist and author of *The Lexus and the Olive Tree*,[1] is the globalizers' new poster boy. Yet even he'll tease out the true intent from the muddled word war. In his book, he cutely describes the investors, corporate planners and pro-business mavericks of today as the "electronic herd" and he offers this analysis of their perception of participatory nations: "The herd is driven to get inside the wiring not because it values democracy per se. It doesn't. It values stability, predictability ... and the ability to transfer and protect its private property from arbitrary or criminal confiscation." In other words, an authoritative, despotic, undemocratic regime is suitable as long as it continues to protect and expand foreign investment activity. Make no mistake, the FTAA (read U.S.A.) accepts undemocratic nations, such as Guatemala and El Salvador. What it will not accept is an un*capitalistic* nation.

Combat Poverty and Inequality

In the U.S. during this supposed economic boom, the income gap has reached record levels with each successive year (1993–2000). Minimum wage is lower now—in real, inflation-adjusted dollars—than it was in 1979. Food bank users have reached record numbers in the last three years. Welfare was trimmed in 1994, an historic repeal of the U.S.'s great social contract. All of this has taken place, I remind you, during one of America's supposed greatest and most prolonged economic booms!

How has Mexico fared since NAFTA? Social spending has decreased—as demanded by the loans orchestrated by the U.S., the IMF and NAFTA after the 1994–95 peso crash—and remains abjectly low. Smog days have increased each year in Mexico City, and income inequality is worse than it's ever been. According to the organization Public Citizen, an additional one million Mexicans work for less than the minimum wage of $3.40 today than before NAFTA.

An editorial piece in the November 30, 2000, edition of *The Washington Post* said it best: "Still, Mexico is an example of globalization-driven growth in more than one way: inequality, already great, has grown worse in the past decade…. Drug trafficking, corruption and violence continue to afflict almost every aspect of civic life, and the abject poverty that spawned the Zapatista rebel movement … remains largely unrelieved." It is significant that this admission appeared in one of the United State's more conservative publications.

Improve Access to Quality Education

Tell that to the kids in city schools. Tell that to any teacher or substitute teacher in the U.S. Ask the teachers and kids who the winner is when corporate interests clash with public needs.

In the U.S., one in four middle and high schools broadcasts Channel One (a ten-minute broadcast that includes two minutes of news and current events and eight minutes of ads and pop-culture gimmicks) to the captivated and prized teen-consumer niche. Marriot, Coca-Cola, Pepsi and other food giants bid for access to halls and dining options. In San Francisco, I saw school buses painted from tip to tail in an Old Navy ad.

Lobbyists have cleverly, and quietly, pushed for years to reduce public funds for education, leaving our districts no choice but to lock into Faustian-like bargains with private industries. And what of quality? Neglect has turned our schools into shopping malls and war zones. Education is a long-term investment that doesn't fit with the short-term, free market approach embodied by the FTAA. Talk of quality improvement holds little promise.

Promote Internationally Recognized Labour Standards, Ensure Safe and Healthy Work Conditions for Migrants

The European Union (EU) allows its citizens to move freely between member states. Vicente

Fox, president of Mexico, proposed to expand NAFTA to include people as well as goods (using the EU as a model). U.S. officials politely laughed his proposal off the table. The Migrant Worker's Convention (MWC) seeks to establish minimum standards for the protection of migrant workers. The problem is that it has lain idle since being introduced in 1993. It requires twenty U.N. countries to ratify the convention, yet only sixteen ratifications exist thus far; all of them are, not surprisingly, majority world countries. The U.S. and Canada continue to deny interest, backed unanimously by other "developed" nations. Patrick Taran, the coordinator for the MWC, smartly explained, "Chile under Pinochet and Iran under the shah did not rush to sign the treaty on torture." The opportunities for us to express our commitment have been present for almost a decade. And we're to believe that suddenly the FTAA agreement will shift our stance.

Respect Human Rights and Fundamental Freedoms

Let's look at our involvement in Central American countries from 1950 to the present. Then again, let's not—it's a rather brutish campaign of human abuses. Even the U.N. passed a resolution rebuking U.S. involvement in Nicaragua in the early and mid-'80s, calling it point-blank, "state-sponsored terrorism."

Now, wouldn't you consider drinking water a fundamental right? This is not under NAFTA, which converted water from a "natural resource" to a "commodity." Water transfers and diversion projects from western Canada (which has 20 percent of the world's fresh water supply) to thirsty golf-course-laden districts in Nevada, Arizona and California are already on the table. He who has the money gets to drink the water—a strange way to respect rights and freedoms, certainly.

California issued legislation to protect its citizens from a carcinogen. "Not so fast!" says NAFTA. California contracted with a Canadian company, Methanex, in the mid-'90s to supply them with a gas additive, MTBE, crucial in assisting them to meet California's strict emission standards. In 1998, the additive was found to be both leaking into water sources at a much higher rate and breaking down much slower than anticipated. In 1999, Governor Davis issued an immediate executive order to begin phasing out this poison, with completion by 2003. Methanex—using NAFTA's notorious Chapter 11 statute—sued California in a NAFTA closed court because the phase-out decision "expropriated their company's profits." In short, investor rights under NAFTA usurp the sovereignty of member nations. Methanex is currently seeking US$1.4 billion in lost profits, based on a $4 to $5 drop in Methanex's stock prices. The same holds true for numerous cases resolved or in the process of being resolved under NAFTA's Chapter 11 (for instance, *Metalclad* vs. *Mexico*, *Ethyl* vs. *Canada*).

Combat Global Drug Problem and Related Crimes

The "war on drugs" wastes tremendous amounts of money and is an affront to our basic freedoms. Consider this: the billion-dollar-plus package of military equipment that the U.S. promised South American countries under Plan Colombia in 2000 will not lessen the "drug crisis." As many South Americans are saying, it will only exacerbate deadly civil wars in the South. If there is a need, there will always be a demand. Try creating a world where the misery of drug usage is no longer viewed as a promising alternative.

Combat AIDS and Its Consequences

This will never happen if it must come at the expense of drug companies' profits! Africa may lose an entire generation to AIDS. The worst estimates indicate that up to 60 percent of the population will be killed within fifty years. India and Brazil produce generic drugs for South Africa, but they have been challenged by U.S. companies both in domestic court and before the WTO. International pressure has achieved some gains; in late March 2001, Bristol Meyers Squibb became the first drug manufacturer to sell two anti-retroviral drugs in combination for just below cost price ($1/day). The move is still a calculated delay; these two drugs are only two-thirds of the cocktail. The third component—absolutely needed to achieve efficacy—is not being offered at such drastic price reductions. The perpetuation of human misery and death for the preservation of profits is appalling. "Intellectual property rights" has become a wonderful, almost lyrical psalm in the global salesmen's bible.

Take Steps to Protect the Environment and Pursue Renewable Resources

I think President Bush said it best. When criticized after pulling the U.S. away from the signatory table of the Kyoto Protocol in 2001, Bush replied, "I will not do anything that may hurt the U.S. economy."

It was some years ago that I first heard a radical take on the United States' arrogant foreign relations endeavours. The profound rawness at which that alternative angle was delivered made me question its legitimacy. "C'mon," I remember thinking, "the U.S. ain't that bad!" I just couldn't reconcile the huge gap between what I had always been told and what was suddenly being revealed. The subject of the lecture was our Central American foreign policy. It was delivered by Noam Chomsky on National Public Radio. This man, one of today's greatest linguists, sparked in me a wonderful search for the truth, the meaning. And what I've found since frightens me. So for anybody reading this who finds its content suspect, I'm not at all surprised. The truth is not blanketed by a few thin sheets but buried deep under thick, down comforters.

We are a generation so conditioned to expect "immediate gains." Results must be readily visible, or we lose hope. But there's reason to remain optimistic. History reveals that we must have patience. Resistance and reform are slow processes that evolve, rippling outward in greater arcs. Our voices have already boomed—now we need to strengthen our alliances, lock arms and hearts and everyday strive to take back that which has been stolen from us. And I suggest we start first with the words.

Educate yourself. Learn what words belong to you and why. And then sing them loud.

Note

1. Thomas Friedman, *The Leaves on The Olive Tree: Understanding Globalization* (Anchor Books, 2000).

An activist on Rue St-Jean prepares to return a tear-gas canister. (Photo: Vincent Pang)

A Generation That Knows the Taste of Tear Gas
Darren Stewart

"The darkest and deepest places in hell are reserved for those who in times of moral crisis refuse to take a stand." —Dante, *The Divine Comedy*

"We want to make sure that every citizen has an equal opportunity to live in dignity."—Prime Minister Jean Chrétien, from his address to the summit delegates during the opening ceremonies.

I spent three days on the frontlines immediately outside the controversial three-metre-high security barrier in Québec City during the Free Trade Area of the Americas meeting. I drove with a group of friends from Toronto and spent fifteen hours each day running between the Indymedia station and the areas of direct-action protest known as red zones. I wielded nothing but a camera and threw only ideas. I filed eyewitness accounts of the action for a conservative talk-radio station in Toronto. I have a journalism background and was aiming for objectivity with my words. This was impossible after what I'd seen and felt in the days previous.

Tear-Gas Dodgeball

The chaos began Friday when the wall came down fast. Tear gas suddenly provided ambiance to the entire city. I breathed it for the first time and gagged. I breathed it through my bandanna for most of the weekend and was myself gassed point-blank more than twenty times while carrying nothing but a water bottle, often far away from violent clashes.

Most TV cameras stuck to the main action and therefore had only one chapter of the story. I spent hours running along the perimeter, sometimes far away from violence, sometimes at ground zero.

The images of the green zones, supposedly designated by protest groups for peaceful protest, are unforgettable—an affront and an assault. A good friend, who came out from Victoria to peacefully protest, was severely gassed early in the day while we were watching the action from a sideline. I helped her into a parking lot, blocks away from the perimeter, for a few moments of peace. She was already incapacitated, gagging and sobbing when police lobbed two more canisters into the parking lot, just to make sure we got the point. Blind and unable to move, she gripped my hand tightly and was forced to hold her face in a filthy snowdrift for several minutes while the second round of gas cleared. My face felt singed behind the barely effective children's swimming goggles and bandanna I was wearing. At this moment, I felt hatred. I wanted to storm the fence and throttle the person who had done this.

I had spent the previous eight months learning and writing about the issues surrounding the FTAA agreement as part of my work in the student press. In Québec, I had many opportunities to use my knowledge to engage people in the streets—protesters and locals alike—on the issues and discover what they felt. On one such occasion I stood well over a hundred yards away from the wall with a group of seniors (including a woman into her seventies) who'd driven from Maine to express their disapproval of the trade agreement. They said they wanted to lend gray-haired credibility to the younger protesters, who are often stereotyped by the mainstream media as young rag-tag anarchists. We stood for a moment in disbelief as two tear-gas canisters suddenly bounced into our midst. With eyes clenched tight we scrambled away around the corner of a building where fellow protesters calmed us and washed our eyes.

"This Is What Democracy Looks Like"

A friend took a photo sequence of a small, unarmed group of protesters who were sitting on the street and holding a placard displaying the peace sign. Police shot a tear-gas canister into their midst. We saw this happen often.

Later, my small group tried to photograph the arrest of two solitary protesters who stood just inside the fence. They had climbed the barrier and were standing their ground, holding an anti-FTAA placard. Moments earlier, and several times before, we'd seen police use brutal force to arrest peaceful and unarmed protesters, particularly those who'd managed to climb the wall with their placards and peace signs. Huge armed and armoured police officers aimed cannons point-blank through the fence and threatened us with them, telling us to stand back and put away the cameras. This was intimidating, especially given the many witness reports we'd heard about police equipment malfunctioning and misfiring throughout the day. Our fear only briefly froze the moment.

With disbelief, I looked through my swimming goggles, through the chain links, into the eyes of police officers one metre away as they lobbed several tear-gas canisters over the fence. They exploded at our feet. I heard the officers' chuckles and taunts as the three of us linked arms and blindly made our way to a safer space. Crying, coughing, noses running and stomachs heaving, we picked our way down the steep streets of Québec, thinking thoughts of democracy. We were trying to document on film police conduct that we didn't believe was right. My friends and I couldn't see for twenty minutes. We couldn't touch our own faces because our hands were covered in gas residue. Fellow protesters rubbed antacids and rubbing alcohol on our burning faces to neutralize the gas. When our raw, red eyes cleared of tears, we headed straight back to the fence for more. We'd come a long way and felt that we were filling a niche beyond that of marching and chanting slogans far away from the action.

Violent/Non-violent

I did not lob any rocks at police, but I often stood nearby and washed the burning eyes of those who did. I refilled my water bottle at a nearby garden hose to wash more eyes and faces. I stood still in the sun and chatted with a middle-aged Québécois man who was wearing no protection against the gas clouds swirling around us. He told me in broken English that he was washing people's eyes as well. He said he couldn't stand to see passionate young protesters suffer for standing up to this. For me this was pure and beautiful, and I shook his hand.

I felt solidarity with Saturday's enormous peaceful march, yet experienced a glowing satisfaction every time I saw people split from the union march to head to the front. I chanted and cheered with many people my parents' age in the red zone. They waved union flags, eyes squinted shut, chanting slogans at the gas-choked frontlines while police officers half their age shot canisters of gas and rubber bullets into their midst.

I do hold onto my mixed feelings about violent protest, even though there were some moments when I was tempted to lob whatever I could back at the police. I remember an incredible moment, when hundreds of protesters, filling an entire city block, sat in the streets metres away from the line of riot police. We sang songs while several people drummed on street signs and danced. The police decided to retreat on the condition that protesters wouldn't advance to the wall again. For nearly an hour, the block was a peaceful swirl of colour and dancing. But the peace was broken suddenly as a cadre of Black Bloc anarchists chose this moment to storm the empty CIBC Bank on the corner and break its windows. The action had a calculated precision and the group left the buildings on either side of the bank intact. Many protesters booed, and some even tried to physically restrain the black-clad group. As the anarchists retreated, one turned back for a moment with a felt marker and wrote on the bank, "Banks don't bleed, protesters have." I agreed and decided that, given how directed, well-orchestrated and symbolic this action was, I supported it wholeheartedly.

Random Acts

This is the point the media has missed entirely: the acts of "violence" undertaken by the more "radical" protest groups were far from random. After lobbing rocks through the windows of a Shell station, someone from the Black Bloc spray painted "Viva Saro-Wiwa" on the station's sign. The anarchists left the neighbouring Esso station intact. Ken Saro-Wiwa (1941–1995) is the Nigerian writer and activist who was hanged on trumped-up murder charges in 1995 after his long campaign against Shell. Many human rights observers maintain that his trial and subsequent sentencing were a farce. Eliminating Wiwa ensured that Shell could keep drilling in Nigeria and filling the coffers of politicians and large multinational corporations. The Shell station hit was not a random act.

Said and Done

My mother, most often conservative and apolitical, sat glued to the TV all weekend, learning much about the issues involved. She was appalled at my story of an innocent friend who was dragged off the street in front of me by police in an unmarked van during the peaceful labour march. (He was later interviewed from jail on CBC about the incident). The charge was "uttering death threats to a police officer," which, upon my soul, is entirely false. My mother got into a heated discussion with a member of her church who said that my friend probably deserved what he got. My friend—political yes, violent no—was doing nothing wrong at the time. He was wearing a motorcycle helmet, ski goggles and a dark jacket and chanting through a bullhorn—neither of which is illegal in this country. His attire was more than appropriate given the random projectiles hurtling through the air from both sides for hours the previous night and the thick cloud of tear gas filling the city. We can only guess that he was targeted because his attire suggested that he could turn "militant" at any moment or incite "violence" in others.

The abduction made a telling point: Who's more to blame for this violence, the taxpayer-funded police and their dangerous arsenal or the protesters fighting back and trying to have their small voice heard? Why should my friend, a passionate believer in socialism and an opponent of capitalism, remain silent? Obviously, he dressed appropriately for the occasion, given the excessive tear gas and the fact that six police officers armed with clubs forcefully abducted him from a public place without warning or good reason.

The weekend in Québec did more to radicalize me than anything I have experienced. No longer will an affinity for used clothes, a refusal to eat fast food, a vegetarian lifestyle and a subscription to Adbusters suffice. I want to buy myself a gas mask, tear this world apart and rebuild it from the roots with others of like mind. After the tear-gas clouds clear and the fence comes down, here stands a radicalized generation.

(Photo: Brandon Constant)

Experiences and Conversation in Québec City

Tullia Marcolongo and Anup Grewal

We went to Québec City as part of a contingent from Trent University and Peterborough, Ontario. Our role was to document the events, Tullia with her camera and Anup with her notepad.

We had worked together before as media contacts and "spindoctors" during a student occupation against corporatization and the undemocratic decision-making processes at our own university. If fact, many of those who have taken action at Trent came to Québec City. As an inside joke, the documentation affinity group named itself "Post-Gzowski" in reference to an article written by Peter Gzowski in the *Globe and Mail* about the politics at Trent.

Upon returning from the protest we read and absorbed many accounts of what had happened in Québec City as presented by mainstream print media and internet sources. It was interesting how our memory of the events became filtered through this media interpretation. We felt we couldn't write anything. In the end, we decided to record a conversation between the two of us to show how we are trying to make sense of the immediate experience and the information we read afterwards.

We chose this format because we feel there is no way to get a *whole* picture of what happened. Like many people, we have only *little* pictures—pictures formed in the numerous and ongoing post-Québec City conversations that are still creating and solidifying the meaning of that event.

Marching Against the FTAA

I remember feeling really jubilant, I was on a kind of high.

I felt the same way, just watching the people amass at the University of Laval, looking at all the costumes and at all the different groups that came. It was a feast for the eyes.

For me it was the colours, the banners, the chants, the slogans and the dancing. It was also that we were all headed towards the fence and we had a common purpose.

I don't know how to fully describe it, but the fact that the Friday march wasn't legally sanctioned gave another kind of feeling because it wasn't what was allowed to happen. It was people wanting to get together and say something. This wasn't Jean Chrétien's "good thing to do"; it wasn't what good protesters were supposed to do.

I remember in the downtown area, as we were getting near the fence, the organizers were telling us we could go to the peaceful green zones now if we don't want to be in yellow actions.

I remember asking you, "Did we make the right choice?" I know I did. But at the time, I started getting this sense of urgency. I wasn't scared yet, I was getting anxious about what would happen and I just continued on.

I felt that too. I also felt this adrenalin. And so many people were ready to face whatever was coming and were willing to challenge the thing that has galvanized this action, the FTAA.

The march wasn't really spontaneous, although sometimes it felt that way. People just came out onto the streets and looked, not knowing what was going on.

Yes, and it wasn't like the second march on Saturday, the legally sanctioned union march, when people were lining the streets. I noticed the difference from the Friday march when people came out of their homes to watch.

The second march felt more like a huge parade. My own involvement in the second march was as an observer. It wasn't something that I felt I was creating.

And we didn't stay long at the second march. What struck me was that it was very colourful. Again there were lots of flags, banners and costumes and people yelling slogans and chants. And I remember passing the Haitian delegation. It was so infectious and lively. They were yelling "Aristide! Aristide!" How strange would it be if people began cheering for "Chrétien! Chrétien!" or even "Trudeau! Trudeau!"

I also wonder, if the huge Saturday march had gone the route of the first march, could a different statement have been made. The fact that it went very far away from the fence said something else.

I only realized later after reading about it and hearing interviews that the second march went away from the fence. It's ironic, especially given that the organizers of the second rally said, "We are in solidarity." I wonder what would have happened if they had gone up to the fence in solidarity with those who were by the fence. I don't know how the police would have responded, maybe their actions would've been less aggressive. But I think it symbolized that there wasn't necessarily solidarity between us. Maybe the "anti-globalization movement" is not cohesive.

Non-cohesion doesn't necessarily have to be negative. There are different ways of being cohesive. I don't think the people who were doing the more confrontational actions were necessarily opposed to people who were marching. But you did see the opposite, some prominent Peoples' Summiters said, "We don't support these violent actions." The media focused so much attention on "violent" actions and took the "good protester/bad protester" line, as did a certain section of the protesters. It made me realize that the people doing so-called "violent" acts were completely marginalized. I think you needed a whole slew of tactics to get into the fence. I think you needed a variety of tactics.

But we needed to work together and not be isolated from each other. On Friday at the fence, there were people who were throwing paint bombs, smoke bombs and concrete slabs. Many others moved back and watched, and a whole mass of people, including me, ran away from the gas because it was so scary. There wasn't much coordination between people ... maybe it was pure spontaneity that brought down the fence, but then what? What would have happened if there had been ... [a plan of action for] after the fence came down?

I wasn't at spokescouncil meetings and, looking back, I would like to have been there to find out more about the finer details of planning. As soon as people started running away from the tear gas, I think that signalled the dispersion of the crowd and the dispersion or the deterioration of the weekend.

I guess the initial euphoria was gone. After everyone was dispersing and we ran down the hill I was thinking, "Okay, is everyone going to gather back?" But it didn't happen. "So what do I do now?" I didn't feel that I was ready to walk up and take on the police by myself; but I thought, "What do I do? What happened to all those people with whom I felt such solidarity?"

I also felt that way. I remember there was a wave of calm right before we went to the fence. When we arrived at the fence the action *really* started and I got so caught up into the whole thing. Suddenly, when the gas really started coming out, I tried not to panic and I went with the crowd, but the crowd started retreating and panicking. I suddenly came down from my euphoria. I felt as though the wind was taken out of me.

The Fence

What about the fence?

I think that there are a lot of different viewpoints about that. People have asked why we were sanctioning "violence," that we didn't have to go to the fence, we could have done something else. And I guess I have asked myself that question too. From the beginning the fence was the focal point, it intensified the protest against the summit. By putting up the fence, the government showed us exactly what they were about and the kind of process that they wanted. It was a very physical symbol. It was something that you had to go up against.

It was a physical barrier and an ideological barrier. It symbolizes so much about how the FTAA is being negotiated and how it excludes so many people. Also, that the documents were not released to the public and still aren't released almost a month after the summit proves their intentions.

Why put a fence up? Logistically, to protect the negotiators and the representatives, but there must be something so fundamentally wrong with this agreement when you have to put yourself behind a fence to negotiate it. The fence incriminates the thirty-four heads of state, and you wonder if they learned from Seattle, Washington and Prague. You don't negotiate behind closed doors and especially not behind a fence. I think it was an affront to my rights to protest and to be in the streets.

They didn't have to put up a fence for the process to be wrong because it was already wrong. And because the fence and the six thousand police were such a violent physical barrier, inevitably you are going to get a "violent" clash. Then they can de-legitimize protesters for having "violent" confrontations, and then protesters can be dispersed. If they didn't put up the fence, it would have been more difficult to dismiss protesters as violent. So they did themselves a bad turn, but they also took public attention away from a lot of the issues.

For most protesters and city residents in the vicinity, the fence was an issue. It was insulting. What if it was my home and I couldn't talk to my neighbour?

From Big Actions to Little Actions

During the big march on Saturday, April 21, we went up to Côte d'Abraham and we saw some major actions where people were trying to pull the fence down. The police started tear gassing and eventually there was some water spraying.

On the second day, I noticed that people were really much more prepared than the first day and I think there was more militancy in the crowd—they were ready for something, they were ready for confrontation. It was like a cat and mouse game though. The crowd trying to get the fence down and police in turn reacting by dispersing the crowd, and then back again. Again, there were a lot of people there, but it was every man and woman for themselves.

There wasn't any concerted action. I did want to participate but I wasn't going to participate like that. I think that's when we started to focus on the back streets, the calmer streets.

But before that we did go up to the huge demo on René-Lévesque, just by the Grand Théâtre. It was another cat and mouse game but it seemed that people were staying a lot more, trying to talk to the police and sitting in. Maybe there was some attempt here at concerted action. It was the same for the sit-in action that night at St-Jean and Côte Ste-Geneviève. Somebody decided to speak up. Somebody decided to say, "Hey, let's sit down." In our own movement at Trent and in Peterborough, I think that at some point I would stand up and say, "Hey everybody, let's come together and rethink." We do that all the time when there is something unexpected going on. But in Québec, I didn't do that.

And that is concerted effort and even though it does seem organized and pre-planned, it wasn't. It was spontaneous—people just sitting down and other people saying, "Yes, I agree with that so let's do it." That is concerted effort.

And that is the way that it has to happen. If we really want to respect a leaderless movement, then it's got to be a movement that has spontaneous leaders that come and then disappear. When someone sees that something is needed, you just do it without an ego … filling a void.

It was unbelievable how cops were terrorizing neighbourhoods and blocking streets. In the back streets they were not protecting the fence, just intimidating people. I didn't see any mainstream media telling us what was happening in the back streets. The police were free to do whatever they wanted because there were very few people watching.

Exactly—sweeping the streets. It made me wonder, "Why didn't we get arrested?" because we were doing exactly the same thing that other arrestees were doing. It shows the complete arbitrariness of the police action. So why should we say that the police were just doing their jobs? Why should we have to make a separation between the state and the police?

At a sit-in on St-Jean on Saturday evening I clearly felt that I could get trampled if the crowd panicked. I was consciously looking for escape routes. I remember that I was thinking I have to pull you up because I wanted you to get out with me.

I felt really odd too. I got really into it, but for the first time, I felt ambivalent about the people who were throwing paint bombs. I felt they were endangering those who were sitting down. I wanted to trust the group, but in the end I couldn't. If the police moved in and the crowd began to panic and run, no one would help me. Panic is horrible.

Debris, Dejection and Determination

I remember going back to Laval on Saturday night and just seeing dejection on people's faces. It was a major change from Friday.

That night walking on St-Jean, there was debris—paper plates, cups, water bottles and discarded this and that…

And so many leaflets! I thought, "Why did we make such a mess of the streets?" We reclaimed the streets and then we trashed them. I was disappointed that people left all the trash. When I think about it, I think we have to recognize our consumer identities, but it's not to say that we all have to suddenly adhere to the same ideals.

Yes, and it becomes an either/or dichotomy. As a protester, you have this identity carved out for you, you're pigeonholed. If you don't conform to the perceived ideal of an activist, it's easy to be de-legitimized.

What do you think of the rhetoric of "war zone?" Québec City was reported as being a war zone in the media. It was a "war zone," but there is also this whole thing of privilege, activism and "summit-hopping" to consider.

Québec City was more in the face of the general public because it was reported as a war zone, but I did get a bit cautious taking away from people who live this in their daily lives; people who are beaten and gassed every single day. I think it was traumatic for a lot of people. You think this could never happen in Canada! But it has and it does. And it happens in so many small ways in different communities. I don't want to take away from this reality by calling Québec City "the affront of affronts," "the war zone of war zones."

Québec made me aware of how the state acts against its own people, its own citizens—at any time and for any reason.

Democracy Or Democracy?

So what about this "Democracy Clause?"

It's an empty promise. How can you have a Democracy Clause when you have a fence? How can you have a Democracy Clause when you have cops terrorizing people? How can you have a Democracy Clause if the relevant documents were not released to the public?

Yes, and how can you have a Democracy Clause when every one of the nations involved in the summit constantly insults anything to do with democracy?

The governments at the summit have a very specific idea of what that democracy means— stability. I'd rather have an FTAA without a Democracy Clause. Such a clause imposes an unethical political ideology on people and it can and has been used in horrible ways. It is, they say, only elected leaders who speak for the people. In the FTAA, democracy solely rests on elections. This view ignores how so many people have a stake in their communities, how so many activists are trying to create ethical societies.

I think people who gathered at Québec City are not only protesters, but they are trying to practise the meaning of democracy. It doesn't always work, but that doesn't mean it should be disregarded. But how do we talk about these attempts? We have citizen-based democracy, we have participatory democracy. W need to talk more so that we can see what are we looking for, what are we asking for?

The FTAA and agreements like it are a manifesto. Democracy has to be lived and practised. Québec showed an organic and flexible movement. We saw this, for example, by participating in the Winnipeg Free Food Kitchen. People working there were doing their own kind of confrontation. They were setting something up that was in direct contradiction to what we are supposed to do as "good" consumers.

Québec radicalized people. I can see here in Peterborough, people are ready to take more action like "Reclaiming The Streets," organizing critical mass bike rides and making links with anti-poverty groups.

So we can't stop. It's not "Let's wait until the next summit to start again." It's "Let's do it now." We'll protest in mass actions, but we'll also continue to make whatever we're trying to make in all its diverse ways. I want to feel like I'm part of something bigger.

It's empowering.

It is empowering. I've always been clear about what I'm not for, what I'm against, and what I am for, as well. But Québec really showed me physically what I'm not for! I'm ready to continue to work for what I have always wanted to do.

It justifies my activism.

What will you remember? A young boy contemplates the police and the fence. (Photo: Steve Daniels)

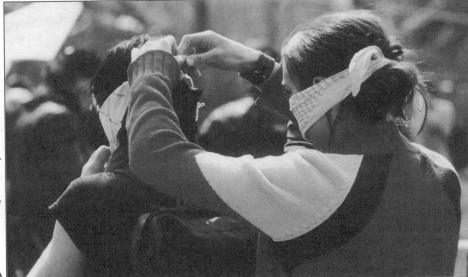

Protesters aid each other by tying on vinegar-soaked bandannas. For many, this was the only protection they had from the ubiquitous tear gas. (Photo: Emmie Tsumura)

An activist assumes a partial change of identity with the aid of a bandanna supplied by one of the affinity groups. (Photo: Mike Kim)

taking it home part

where to go from here

Women Talking About Sexism in the Anti-Globalization Movement[1]

Caitlin Hewitt-White

As activists who are committed to fighting global capitalism, we often erroneously posit oppression as a phenomenon that we can fight because it is not part of who we are. There seems to be an assumption at work that if we are fighting "the system" that is oppressive, then we are somehow "nonoppressive" by virtue of claiming to be "outside" of the system. None of us are immune from the grasp of patriarchy, racism and homophobia. The implications of thinking that we are immune can dangerously affect the participation of systemically oppressed peoples in the movement and can significantly limit the revolutionary potential of our work.

Over the past seven months, I have been compiling women's ideas about gender, sexism and oppression within what is known as the "anti-globalization movement" in North America, characterized as it is by mass actions dominated by young, white people, mostly of middle-class privilege. In doing this, I wanted to look at how activists behave in gendered ways; how sexism within activism arises; and how sexism is intertwined with other oppressions, such as racism and heterosexism. Over twenty women from across Canada have invested hours of thought and work into this project. The women are currently active within popular education and direct action groups fighting corporate globalization. Most women who participated are white, lesbian, bi or queer and able-bodied. About a quarter of the participants are women of colour; two Jewish women and one Aboriginal woman participated. Most of the women identify themselves as having queer-positive, feminist, radical, anti-authoritarian politics.

Covert Oppression

Oppression in activism, as in North American society in general, functions systemically, often in covert and subtle ways. Most oppressive behaviour is often difficult to notice and confront while it is actually happening. In anti-globalization activism in Canada, uncritical gendered behaviour is manifesting itself in ways that limit women's potential to self-determine the degree of fulfilment they get out of their activism. Sexism in the movement is made manifest in the gendered division of labour, the amount of power accorded to men's voices over those of women and in overtly sexist behaviour, such as harassment and assault. Sexism intertwines with other oppressions, such as racism and classism, to systemically exclude women of colour and women with little or no income.

Division of Labour

I found that the type of work women are taking on in their activist communities is deeply shaped by gendered socialization. Women tend to spend a lot of their time facilitating, training and skill-sharing, as well as planning actions. Although the women I spoke to sometimes see women taking on these types of work more than men, what makes these roles gendered is the set of skills required for these roles that women, not men, are socialized to have.

For instance, action planning is carried out in gendered ways within the movement. Sarah spoke to me of her experience becoming involved in an occupation of a university's administrative offices as protest against its privatization. The campaign unofficially began with a group of men planning apparently "radical" actions, such as spray painting over university signs. The men drifted away when more people became involved and serious discussion of an occupation unfolded. "It ended up being women who were really committed to it and who were willing to address those risks: jail solidarity, group dynamics, talking about what our fears were and those types of things," she explained. "We were really concerned about people's feelings and the emotional impact of our actions." When the occupation happened and generated national media attention some men became involved again for various reasons. One reason was the gendered way in which men gravitate towards immediately public, visible, vocal and self-affirming actions and roles.

Traditionally, female-dominated work is overwhelmingly performed by women in the movement. The women I spoke with see mostly women taking on the clerical or reproductive tasks, such as note-taking, childcare, typing, food preparation and phone calls. Furthermore, traditionally, male-dominated work is still being done by men. Women told me that web-based work, acting as a spokesperson and public speaking and education are the most male-dominated types of work in the movement. Despite this, many of the women are resisting gendered barriers to doing work that they enjoy by doing this work too. Web-based work is the exception; very few women are working in this area, although they want to. Because the vast majority of anti-globalization mobilizations are coordinated and publicized via websites and e-mail list-serves, the lack of women's web-based work means that men dominate a huge amount of networking between anti-globalization groups.

Women's motivation to do the work they do is also often gendered. Although more than half of the women I spoke to are doing work that they decide for themselves they want to do, the majority also told me that they "pick up" tasks they fear won't get done if they don't do them, a fear not often shared by men.

The gendered expectation of women to be more emotionally driven, nurturing and communicative than men is being reproduced in activist spaces. Women are socialized to sense other people's feelings, to do last-minute tasks, to pick up the slack and to not let our lack of pleasure in doing these things stand as reason for discontinuing to do them. Although men can indeed possess these skills as well, the experience of women in this project indicates that they are more likely to make use of these traditionally female-gendered skills in their anti-globalization activism than are men. Women in anti-globalization activism still face structural gendered barriers to accessing certain skills that are mostly possessed by men with time, money and an apparent unwillingness to share their skills on a collective scale. Many men are actively and passively perpetuating this division of labour; they benefit from it insofar as it helps them focus on the work they enjoy the most.

Voice

Most of the women I spoke with are active in anti-globalization groups that have a roughly equitable representation of women. In the anti-hierarchical, anti-authoritarian spirit of the movement, many groups use consensus decision-making, which theoretically allows for the equal and free participation of everyone present. Despite this structure, which is intended to equalize power, most of the women I spoke with feel that men still tend to speak up the most at meetings. Even if men and women speak up an equal number of times, men are more likely to repeat what has already been said and to talk longer. They are also more willing to get off topic and not be brought back to the focus of the discussion, and they are taken more seriously than are women.

The result of men taking up space is that many women feel uncomfortable in male-dominated settings. Many of the women feel "intimidated" and fear being "shot down" more than they do in women-dominated settings.

Not only men tend to silence women; nor are women only silenced because of sexism. For women of colour, the experience of being silenced stems from intertwined racism and sexism. Zee, a woman of colour, told me of an incident at a women's centre that she feels is representative of racist silencing in many forms of activism in general. A white co-worker would always ask her a question about her opinions or her work only to "invariably talk right over" her. Two white women initially sympathized with the woman who was being silenced, yet never ended up confronting the silencing co-worker themselves.

Exclusion

Most of the respondents told me that they have experienced or have seen the effects of oppressive assumptions and attitudes among anti-globalization activists. Some women referred to instances in which oppressive assumptions have been vocally expressed. For instance, a queer woman reported that other activists always make comments expressive of the heterosexist assumption that she is straight.

Some women told me that oppressive assumptions are usually unspoken but underlie the entire operation of activist groups. Exclusion is often structural rather than the result of an outright action that prohibits or bars participation. Activist groups sometimes do not actively encourage and facilitate the participation of people who face systemic barriers to participation. As a white woman explained to me, many groups do not actively encourage the participation of women or people of colour because they are operating on the assumption that if women or people of colour want to participate, nothing is holding them back.

People of low or no income and people who are not students probably have less access to information about anti-globalization organizing than do students or activists of middle-class privilege who own or have access to shared computers with internet service. The costs of attending a protest quickly rack up: the cost of taking time from work and family responsibilities, transportation to the protest and within the city, food and potentially bail and other legal costs incurred in an arrest situation. People of colour who are routinely the targets of police brutality are more at risk during confrontational actions than are white people. The institutionalized sexism and queerphobia of the state is likely to violently bear down more on women, transfolk and queer people once they are detained. Rarely are these risks even mentioned in legal and direct action trainings. At three such trainings that I know of at the FTAA protests in Québec City, these risks were brought up by female workshop participants rather than by the workshop facilitators.

When I asked women in interviews for other examples of exclusion, many simply replied that they know of many radical women and people of colour who do not participate in the "anti-globalization movement." They do not feel compelled to because it is dominated by white people who often do not address their own oppressive behaviour or the ways in which systems of oppression are used by and facilitate capitalism. Add to this the general problem among many activists of not supporting the ongoing anti-poverty, anti-racist campaigns in which many people of colour and those living in poverty are already involved by virtue of simply struggling to survive the impoverishing effects of neocolonial capitalism.

Overt Oppression

Overt sexism and oppression do indeed happen in the movement in ways that many people often assume "just do not happen anymore." Roughly one fifth of the women I spoke with reported experiencing or knowing of oppressive jokes and harassment occurring in activist spaces. For instance, one woman spoke of an incident wherein a male organizer made a joke about her sexuality at a large organizing meeting.

Because of the assumption that assault is a more pernicious yet less rampant form of oppression than others, and because speaking of assault is still so systemically stigmatized, some activists may be alarmed to hear that 9 percent of the women in this project either had been assaulted in an activist setting or know another woman who had. Women spoke of situations involving sexual assault or sexual objectification and harassment bordering on assault between partners or acquaintances who were both active in the same activist community. In some cases people within an organization had discovered that one activist had assaulted a woman or women in the past but they never resolved how to deal with the aggressor.

What is surprising is not so much the frequency of assault within activist communities, which I think is typical in any community as we all live within a patriarchal system wherein violence against women is the norm. What I find most disappointing is the apparent lack of structures and effort to collectively decide how to support survivors on the one hand and how to hold abusers accountable on the other. One woman who was at an anti-globalization conference where a man had attempted to assault a woman suggested that having women-only safe spaces at overnight events would help prevent a similar situation in the future. Another woman complained of how one anti-globalization organization had "exploded" upon discovering that an abuser was in its midst, and how policies around the inclusion or exclusion of abusers in such organizations would have helped. It is here where I think feminist sensibility would be most useful to anti-globalization activists and where some parts of the movement's lack of reconstructive vision is harming women. Such a vision could articulate not only what we are presumably resisting: patriarchy, capitalism and oppression. It could also articulate what we want to build: a society in which aggressors are held accountable for their actions and women are safe from sexist aggression in their own communities.

Women's Demands for Anti-Oppression Strategizing

There remains a tremendous amount of resistance to dealing with oppression in activist communities. Backlash, denial and an unwillingness to strategize ways to deal with oppression compound the initial experiences of sexism and oppression for the women involved. As a result, many feel further silenced and alienated from their own communities. I asked women how oppression is usually addressed and what they want to see change.

Most women reported that once an oppressive incident occurs in activist settings there is some degree of one-on-one confrontation between the affected woman and the perpetrator. However, in very few cases would the perpetrator respond positively or change their behaviour in a committed and consistent way.

The second most common way that women deal with sexism and oppression against themselves or other women by is doing nothing at all. Reasons for this include not feeling safe or supported enough by others. Many women also did not realize that what had happened was oppressive or warranted intervention until after the fact. This was especially true for cases involving subtle dynamics for which it is difficult to find descriptive language. Once they realized it, "not wanting to rock the boat" or not wanting to cause "interpersonal difficulties" kept them from taking action. Fear of backlash dominates women's decisions about addressing oppression.

As in life in general, women use a variety of ways to cope with and resist sexism and oppression. Many women activists told me of venting to other women about their concerns and experiences, focusing on supporting victims and survivors or ending friendships with perpetrators of oppressive actions. A few women are currently withdrawing from mixed-gender activism and focusing more on woman-centred or explicitly feminist activism directly because of their frustration with sexism and oppression in the movement.

Women and people of colour are too often left alone with the sometimes unsafe burden of confronting their oppressors without support, especially from people of privilege. People of privilege can and ought to be committed to a political position that both refuses to perpetuate oppression and attempts to dismantle it. This commitment has to be combined with the desire to be held accountable for the oppressions in which people of privilege are implicated. Men and white people benefit from and are shaped by systemic oppressions; the best intentions will not erase this. Activists must collectively devote the time and energy plus find the resources to empower themselves and others to intervene in situations of injustice, inequality and oppression among activists.

There ought to be support structures and networks, informal or formal, in place for people who decide to confront a perpetrator of oppression. Groups must do much more than just check in to see how a confronter is feeling about the issue or incident three weeks later. Take direction from the person most affected by the oppressive behaviour. Ask them how you can best help them establish safe space to vent, receive support and challenge oppression. Safe spaces sometimes means women-only or people-of-colour-only spaces. If you are not welcome in such a place, listen to the stated reasons why or figure it out for yourself, and please be supportive of it.

Education and Awareness

Informal approaches to oppression, or no approach at all, prevail among activists and usually go hand-in-hand with a glaring lack of anti-oppression policies. Less than half of the women said that their anti-globalization group had some form of explicitly stated anti-patriarchal, anti-sexist, pro-feminist, anti-discriminatory or anti-oppressive principles entrenched in their group's mandate. Women who belong to groups that have no such principles explained that their newly-formed group either had a mandate that was restricted to "mobilizing for the FTAA" (as though the FTAA does not have racist or sexist implications) or had not yet come up with any mandate at all.

Developing mandates and policy in hopes of helping to create a political culture of resistance to oppression is a pipe dream if basic discussions about oppression and sexism are not happening in the first place. Most of the women belong to groups that have had some form of general anti-oppression training, yet less than half of these groups use educational tools specifically aimed at fighting racism, sexism, homophobia heterosexism and transphobia.

Women explained this lack of anti-oppression educational strategies as being a result of insufficient interest. Others pointed to the lack of resources that tends to plague grassroots groups in general (yet has not prevented activists from renting buses and trains to get to mass actions like in Québec City). Most women simply replied that their focus is on "globalization," not oppression, as though the two were separable.

Women's Visions for the Movement

When I asked women what their vision was for the movement, some sighed, some groaned, some rubbed their head as though they were in great pain and others laughed. Some pointed to one or two examples of certain teach-ins that have put colonialism, patriarchy and racism at the centre of the discussion. Nearly all of the women referred to the Colours of Resistance network that has recently formed and that attempts to build relationships among communities directly struggling to cope with the brutal effects of capitalist globalization and the more white-dominated, mainstream "anti-globalization movement." Nearly all of the women also referred to Elizabeth "Betita" Martinez's article "Where Was the Color in Seattle?"[2] as another example of how anti-racist, anti-colonial discourse is becoming more integrated into the "movement." "Stick It to the Manarchy," written by feminist/pro-feminist anarchists in the U.S., and other recent pieces that directly address the gendered nature of some apparently male-dominated actions have circulated among anti-globalization activists and have generated some discussion, if only over e-mail list-serves.

However, the experiences of the women who participated in this project show that there must be more sustained and collective effort to fully integrate an anti-sexist, anti-racist, anti-oppressive analysis into the "anti-globalization movement." We ought to make the links among various systems of oppression as they operate both "outside" of the movement in the capitalist system we oppose as well as within our very own activist communities.

If there was a general consensus among the women I spoke with as to what they want to see happen in the "anti-globalization movement," especially after Québec City, it could be summed up like this: "Sustainable community-building, not summit-hopping!" Summit-hopping is draining, prohibitively expensive and inaccessible to many people (especially those who are directly affected by capitalist globalization) and presently dominated by white students from a middle-class background. The women I spoke with are keenly aware that anti-globalization activism burns people out, especially women who tend to pick up the slack created by men. Burnout is not sexy or revolutionary. They recognize that constant, large-scale, action-intensive, risk-laden mobilization sometimes wreaks havoc on their hearts, bodies and relationships.

Part of making anti-globalization activism more accessible and being able to make the time and devote the energy to solidarity work is making activism healthier. Many women told me that they want to see more sharing of work and more activists emotionally and logistically supporting each other inside and outside of activist projects. Sharing work includes people of privilege taking on a more active role in confronting oppression in activism.

There are grassroots activist organizations popping up across North America that have little more on their agenda than getting people with similar identities or lifestyles to the next mass demonstration. An opposition to corporatization is often the common link among activists, especially for people who have just recently become politicized by the anti-globalization movement itself. An opposition to racism, sexism, capitalism and other systems of domination is rarely integrated into the goals of these new, temporary, action-oriented anti-globalization groups.

The women I spoke with expressed a deep desire to refocus their energies on the effects of capitalist globalization in their own communities and to stand in solidarity with communities most directly affected by capitalism. Most want to build meaningful relationships with Aboriginal communities, communities of colour and low-income communities by engaging in frontline work or by supporting their ongoing struggles. To do this, organizations must become more sustainable, accessible, self-reflective, clear about their mandate and established in their communities.

The sort of political dialogue aimed at articulating a vision of what we are fighting for should not wait until after the next action. We can start developing a vision of how we want the world to be by simply observing gender, race and power dynamics around us. In our own activist organizing and at the next action we can ask ourselves: Who is speaking to the media? Who is being affected by our actions as demonstrators? Who didn't come to the protest and why not? Is this what we want a post-revolutionary world to look like?

The web of oppressive systems will lose legitimacy and will start to crumble when both beneficiaries and survivors of oppression build a truly democratic countersociety where every instance of domination and oppression is confronted consistently, effectively and ethically. We ought to seriously look at how the systems we want to fight are reproduced in ourselves, in our relationships and in our communities.

Notes

1. An expanded version of this article appeared in *Kick It Over*, Issue Number 39 (June 2001). Thanks to all of the women who directly participated in the project, for all the time they devoted to participating as well as for feedback and encouragement along the way. Thanks to Marc Bernhard for last-minute editorial assistance. This piece was based on research generously funded by the Institute for Anarchist Studies.
2. Elizabeth "Betita" Martinez, "Where Was the Colour in Seattle? Looking for Reasons Why the Great Battle Was So White," Spring 2000, *www.tao.ca/~colours*

(Photo: Brandon Constant)

Living Earth

Anon Ymous

in our hurry to consume,
we hurt our friends

how did violence and
warfare chemicals affect
the birds and other animals who
live in Québec City?

in our hurry to control
we poison our food

when we mess with the
life giving seed,
how long will we be around?

Poomy Thai (Earth)
can take care of herself,
in our crusades to save our own skin
how aware are we of our fellow beings?

when will we learn to look inside
to know where we belong?

when will we look past our arrogance,
to see beauty in all living beings?

Under

Ladner Reet

combat boots seen from Under the table
where we were holding hands hiding
grabbed by the hair
this strong body
emerged limp
go limp or they'll get you for resisting arrest and assaulting a puppet
you have to
submit to the man's
exalted cigar breath
(where's Cuba?)
exhaling the words
"squash the resistance,
those destroying a very good democracy"
with chrétien complimentary
tactics of violence
that never made victims of us
but instead breaks any identity crisis
the supposed bland bondage of no-culture, no-place, no-relations
we know what we are made of, have the struggle,
the reason, le locale, the fighting of off coca-cola-nizations and
global puss-spewing contests
grannies raging, children running
we unite Under the stars we are made of
and Under the plump thumb of the lonely leaders
who dress their own wounds
ten million times
before scouring at the surface of problem solving
keeping love in hand cuffs
we love frogs, trees, papillons, boats, phasms, oxygen, daydreams and
daydreamers, ocean waves and wavelets, green, natural sheen, and each other.
who can love money and reach
  satisfaction
    fulfilment,
      and
        Understanding, truth and peace?

(Photo: Brandon Constant)

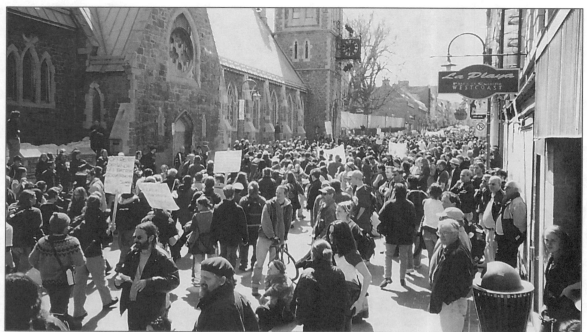

(Photo: Tricia Bell)

(Photo: Jo-Anne McArthur)

Rebuilding the Global Rebellion

Kagiso Molope

Shortly before his death in 1965, Malcolm X travelled to North Africa and Europe where he watched Black people from diverse backgrounds join forces and fight racial prejudice. He was amazed at how people from different parts of the world could be engaged in the same battle and at how much power there could be in solidarity. Upon his return to North America, he referred to this struggle against racism as a "global rebellion"—it was one of the most empowering experiences for X. At first glance, we may see the so-called "anti-globalization movement" as something that seems to fit the idea of a "global rebellion," since it consists of activists from around the world. And it really has been invigorating to watch thousands of people put so much energy into this fight against the WTO, the World Bank, the IMF and the FTAA. From now on, Seattle, D.C., Melbourne and Québec will always remind us of what happens when people form a united front and insist on being heard. So, at first glance, it looks hopeful.

However, upon taking a further look, it is hard not to notice the segregation that exists within the "anti-globalization" movement. I have found it hard to stay within activist circles that oppose the FTAA and capitalist globalization in general because often I've been the only person of colour, and there was no space to discuss or work on the racism that existed within this circle of activists. It still feels like there is as much a need for a unified force of people of colour (not just people of African origin) fighting racism in Canada as there was in the U.S.— and all over the world—in 1965. This is really disconcerting since we all have a common cause and could work well together if the systemic barriers within activist groups were effectively dismantled.

A week before people were going to Québec, I watched a television report about a Ruckus Society activist camp in the U.S. At first, I was really pleased that the media was actually taking the time to hear from young activists, giving them a chance to have their say. But thirty minutes into the TV special, I was losing my patience and couldn't understand why. Then I realized that almost everyone in the camp was white, and of the people of colour present not one was interviewed or captured for a length of time by the camera. It is an all too familiar picture. What most of us don't realize is that it is at times like these that the division between us becomes more apparent. Repeating the common discourse, the activists interviewed at the camp mentioned nothing about their concerns about the Global South and seemed not to question the racial dynamics of their group.

However, even if the mainstream media is not taking the time to hear what people of colour have to say, there is little doubt that the global struggle against capitalism has everything to do with racism. But as usual, the media chooses to see human rights violations in the majority of the world and racism as separate issues, as if they are mutually exclusive. Racism once again takes a back seat to what the white-dominated media considers important.

If we are to speak of all of the effects that the FTAA will have on us and how it will decrease already declining living standards, let's speak frankly of the great power imbalance between North and South America, the already existing exploitation of Mexican migrant workers and the very fact that thousands of refugees fleeing horrific economic conditions enter Canada and the U.S. every day from all countries south of the U.S. border. Let's point out that these things are true not only because these people are victims of North American capitalist greed but also because these people *are* people of colour whose lives are grossly undervalued. The majority of people in these countries are living in poverty, and it is important to point out who "the poor" on a global spectrum are—they are people of colour.

There is a misunderstanding of and discrimination towards people of colour who flee their countries, especially when North Americans have not yet heard of the declared war or genocide happening in the country from which they are fleeing. Canadians often see these refugees as "coming to take our jobs." Canada currently does not accept refugees from several countries whose claims are based on economic reasons. Among these countries are Mexico and Ghana. What do these two share in common? Canada and the U.S. are two of their largest investors. So, the logic follows: if Canada and the U.S. accept refugees from those countries, they will be admitting to playing some part in the exploitation/repression of their peoples.

When corporations close down businesses in northern countries and go out in search of cheap labour, they turn inevitably to countries largely populated by people of colour where they can easily exploit and disregard human rights. This only increases with the implementation of any free trade agreement. And since countries and corporations that benefit from agreements such as the FTAA will not be required to respect human and environmental rights in southern countries, we can expect to see even more environmental and social degradation in the Global South.

It is disturbing that we are not a unified group and that even in this struggle, to which we all have something to contribute and in which only masses can bring about change, we cannot be one. On this point, some white people tend to get angry, pointing out that this is not about racism and then going on to talk about labour and the environment. But it's really about all of these issues and more! It has come to a point at which many white people won't listen if you say "race" and many people of colour walk away when you say "environment."

Within any movement for social justice there has to be mutual respect among people. We have to be able to keep our eyes on our common goals because our chances at success are always greater if we are united. At this point we are faced with fighting corporations and heads of state, none of whom have our best interest at heart—our rights have already been grossly violated. So this is a struggle that calls for a new "global rebellion," and in this age that means white people and people of colour coming together. If that is to happen we have to be able to hear each other, work on our prejudices and then present ourselves as a unified force.

In search of the best views, photographers attempt to cover every angle. (Photo: Emmie Tsumura)

Student march, Saturday, April 21. (Photo: Erin George)

Lest We Forget?

Anon Ymous

To Québec City
most went with hope
and talk of revolution
poison was breathed
state sanctioned brutality witnessed
and then went home to be relieved

In many places
millions live with
hope and death
all around them
but home for them
is the place of an
on going revolution

In Québec
eyes were opened
some of the privileged
were shook
still the exploitative
conveniences of life
remain intact
how far from your
backyard is the revolution?

Bondage Free

Gian Mura

Greed and corporations
make our lives abominations
clear cuts scar the face of Gaia
pollution, an accepted way to die.
We have not the right to speak
police barricades everywhere,
protect pesky billionaires.
Sterile environments are no solution
cement is no acceptable substitution
to butterflies dancing on fields of flowers
or rays of sunshine, playing diamonds on cool waters.
Our children's children have the right to see
the canopy of a forest
made up of thousand years old trees.
For this we fight today
so common sense prevails
to shape tomorrow's ways.

Under a "Welcome" banner, workers barricade a business down in the new city. (Photo: Steve Daniels)

Anti-Racist Organizing: Reflecting on Lessons from Québec City

Pauline Hwang

"Parlez francais ici, hostie! Go back your country! Go back your country! *C'est mon pays, pas ton pays."* Translation: "Speak French here, &%$/★! Go back to your country! This is my country, not your country."

These are the words that a Montréal activist of colour heard from riot police, who were beating and choking him during April's demonstrations against the Summit of the Americas in Québec City. Another prominent activist, Jaggi Singh, was singled out as a leader, kidnapped and beaten—in part because police say his so-called "Hindu origin" made him easily noticeable. Police intimidation also helped divert a planned alternative summit on Indigenous Peoples and the Free Trade Area of the Americas (FTAA), according to organizer Tony Hall.

The blatantly racist police repression at summit protests is one reason that these mass mobilizations have not represented most First Nations activists or activists of colour—a point made over and over by these activists. Unfortunately, it is not the only reason. Subtler systemic racial exclusion in our organizing is still present.[1] Those of us in Québec had hoped that lessons learned since Seattle would have changed the face of the Québec City mobilization. But despite all the hard and exciting work that went into the event, we still seem to have a long way to go in developing anti-racist, multiracial organizing.

Helping to organize against the FTAA made clear to me how difficult and crucial it is to close the gap between radical anti-racist theory and practice. Many activists may see "globalization" as a newer version of the centuries-long, racialized, imperialist project to exploit the vast majority of peoples and environments. The fight against globalization is not just a hope to reverse "corporate rule" but a long, international struggle for full social, economic and environmental justice.

Here, however, I wanted to reflect on race issues in the process of organizing not in the content of issues raised, though both are important and related. I mostly organize with the Shakti women of colour collective, the Immigrant Workers' Centre and a loose coalition of other Montréal-area community groups. For the anti-FTAA protests, I was also a member of a campus-based FTAA-Alert. The campus and community experiences were very different.

Though many activists have been introduced to anti-oppression principles, some still don't see them as central to social change and still others, myself included, must challenge ourselves further to apply these principles to our everyday practice. I echo Helen Luu's point:

> A movement that is dedicated to bringing down all forms of oppression simultane-
> ously with challenging global capitalism is the kind of movement we must endeavour

to work towards, if we are truly serious about fighting for a world that is free and just for all.[2]

Setting the Scene

On campus, anti-FTAA publicity was massive, well-resourced and successful. Hundreds of students jumped on the anti-FTAA bandwagon. Groups at McGill University alone pitched in over $3500. But if we had called a people of colour caucus among the organizers, the members could have been counted on one hand. Other central organizing groups, such as FTAA-Alert Concordia, Groupe Opposé à la Mondialisation des Marchés (GOMM), SalAMI and even the Anti-Capitalist Convergence, consisted largely of white activists, including many campus-based activists. This is not to say that other groups were not interested in or preparing for the demonstrations; but they were not, for whatever reason, part of the central coordination and planning of the demo.

In fact, the monochrome organizing wasn't a surprise. The activist scene here in Montréal is already somewhat divided along linguistic (English/French) and ideological ("violence/ nonviolence") lines. And, in general, Québec is still struggling (perhaps that is an understatement) to reconcile "multiculturalism" with its nationalist project to counter historic British imperialism. So not only is racism strong in Québec, but addressing both the original colonization of First Nations' land and the more recent racist immigration policies has political complications unique to Québec. It is difficult to bring folks together to talk about anything, never mind to self-reflect on racism in progressive movements. (These aren't excuses, just context.)

One of the strengths of this recent North American "anti-globalization movement" is that it's drawn from various established movements—labour, environment, human rights, feminist groups, students against sweatshops, etc. However, this particular strength comes with its difficulties: many of these movements have not yet fully addressed the structural racism, not to mention many other forms of oppression, historically present within them.

In my experience, this means racial exclusion and oppression in anti-FTAA coalitions. For example, a woman in a "feminist" space told me that "people of colour just need to get involved" and that "we" should "stop complaining [about the racism in the group] and do something about it." When I objected to what this woman said, she described me as "overreacting and susceptible." Elsewhere, I was told that the off-campus issues on which I was working were not "directly related to globalization"; I suppose because they weren't directly mobilizing college students to hit the streets, which is how many have come to define the "anti-globalization movement." In addition to blatant comments such as these, our group of people of colour and immigrant workers faced more structural challenges to meaningful participation in Québec.

Mobilizing Communities of Colour

Some groups started to form a loose coalition/caucus among communities of colour opposing imperialist globalization. We had networking meetings and community forums and we made links with labour and immigration struggles. But this time spent on explicitly "anti-globalization" work was limited because of more immediate campaigns.

At first our coalition/caucus had hoped at least to share our demands at the Peoples' Summit. However, it took place during the week when no one could afford to miss work and abandon children and family to "represent" the group. For similar reasons, we could go to Québec City only on Saturday, and even then many people could not make it. Moreover, we had no control over the bus schedule and ended up being in Québec so briefly that we could not rally with the people-of-colour contingent from Toronto and elsewhere; in fact, we spent most of the time looking for each other, having been sent in two separate buses. Because of the physical and legal danger near the security perimeter, we attended the legal march, which was a long walk to a distant stadium. Despite our safety precautions, however, some youth of colour dropped out at the last minute—likely because of expected police violence and/or Friday's TV coverage of excessive police force.

I say all this not to complain but because it struck me how difficult it was to fully enjoy a mobilization seemingly designed for and managed by particular types of activists. As activist/writer Chris Dixon points out:

> A key problem, then, with the focus on mass mobilizations is the underlying idea that we, as people who seek radical social change, must each take great risks and make huge commitments in very prescribed ways—and that all of us can afford to do that. Yet this just doesn't face reality.[3]

We were also at odds with many other groups because we couldn't put all our energy into Québec City. If we had been able to do so, we could have mobilized even more people and raised more money. Luckily, some community organizers kept their perspective on local issues, choosing to reserve resources for necessary ongoing work. But last-minute calls for funding for the mass mobilization caused activist groups to shell out big money, some of which we received but ironically probably could not have accessed for ongoing campaigns. I'm glad the mobilization was a success. I also can't help thinking about the incredible difference that even half those resources, energy and people power could make if invested in local, shoestring-budget campaigns that are also fighting globalization, though differently.

The Dynamics of Inclusion

My conversations with community organizers before and after Québec City reveal problems with basing the "movement" in groups that have historically alienated and poorly represented "marginalized" communities, particularly because many members still have trouble listening nondefensively to these criticisms. Some admitted to being both turned off from the get-go and uninspired by actions and tactics that seem so exciting for mostly white, male, middle-class activists but that have little sense of equal partnership. Some feel unrepresented by the spokespeople and writers who are said to speak for the movement; they don't want to be "special interest groups," lobbying the movement to include "our" issues. Others often must work with problematic and oppressive "allies" and must spend time and energy fighting racism within activist groups when they could be mobilizing in the community. Those who must still appease members who control the resources—while also doing the anti-oppression education so that the work we do will be validated, recognized and funded—are tired of being accused of "identity politics" or of being "dismissed as soft, bitchy, counter-revolutionary or PC." Some are caught between wanting to demonstrate radical opposition to global capitalism and needing to protect their safety, legal status, job and earnings, family, health, etc. Others prefer changing socioeconomic realities to debating ideology.

As Jane G., a volunteer with New York's Coalition for the Human Rights of Immigrants, puts it:

> Inclusion obviously means different things to different people. To some it means throwing the doors open to everyone, without any kind of structured plan for involving groups who so far have been disenfranchised from the entire process. This kind of "inclusion" inevitably means that discussion and decision-making will be dominated by 1) those who have e-mail and know about it; 2) those who have the resources (time and money) to get there; 3) those who feel their opinion is more important and are therefore most comfortable dominating the conversations; etc. This type of "inclusiveness" almost guarantees a lack of diversity which will be very hard to reverse later, since those few groups from outside this elite privileged clique who decide to give the process a chance will quickly be driven out when they see the dynamic. [4]

Before the summit, anti-oppression work we did with campus-based groups helped make some improvements. Allies, on whose shoulders I could cry when frustrated, helped us in urgent situations to get quicker respect and resources. Some students began to see the racialization of the globalization process, at least enough to say "capitalist globalization is racist!" Several members began attending events, such as "Women of Colour Resisting Imperialism" and demonstrations against the deportation of a former live-in caregiver whose only crime was to get pregnant. Fewer still saw the links to the fight for Africana Studies and other long-term anti-racist work. Outside of Québec, one exciting idea was the border crossing at Akwesasne, Mohawk territory. It was a creative direct action—i.e., thinking outside the "shut down the Summit" box, asserting First Nations sovereignty and addressing border enforcement—not only for protesters, but for all people.

Talking the Talk

Perhaps it is a sign of progress that other groups have begun referring to globalization's racialized impact in statements, principles and reports. The final declaration of the Peoples' Summit of the Americas (a parallel NGO summit) stated that "this neo-liberal project is racist and sexist." The Canadian Federation of Students (CFS) has put out a fact sheet entitled "Is Globalisation Colour Blind?" The Centre for Social Justice published a report on Canada's Economic Apartheid, which was featured on CBC TV's *Counterspin*; it's funny how communities of colour have noticed the inequity for years, but it didn't make prime time TV then. Montréal's GOMM referred to racism and other oppressions under their "feminist" demands. Even groups like the Council of Canadians appear to be slowly changing their official line on racism.

At FTAA-Alert, we stuck a clause saying the group was "anti-sexist, anti-racist and anti-homophobic" into the mandate and managed to rid the group of a white supremacist who was stirring up the e-mail list. But it seemed difficult enough to combat this blatant discrimination, never mind the daily organizing habits that made the group inaccessible.

However, few activists challenged and continue to challenge subtle, internal racism within ourselves and our groups beyond openly noting the lack of "diversity." The groups mentioned above have been heavily dominated by white, middle-class activists and have not addressed the racial exclusivity in ongoing work, including anti-FTAA organizing. That is not to say that these groups have not done good work, but to point out areas in which we still need to work.

So Where Are We Going and How Can We Get There?

The call-out for "A Critical Dialogue on Confronting Oppression Within Activist and 'Alternative' Communities" says bluntly:

> While activists rush back and forth across the continent looking for the next big event, important questions remain unanswered and complicated internal conflicts lurk in the dark corners and closets of our communities. Why is it never the right time or place to acknowledge or confront the rampant sexism, racism, homophobia, and arrogance within supposedly radical organizations?[5]

According to the Colours of Resistance statement, we "are committed to helping build an anti-racist, anti-imperialist, multiracial, feminist, queer liberationist, and anti-authoritarian movement against global capitalism." In other words, we envision and work towards ending social oppressions as well as the global capitalism that both supports them and is supported by them. But this requires time for listening, learning, serious mutual critiques and long-term visioning.

Most groups are much more willing to talk about racialized globalization on the international level, agreeing that developing countries are hurt most by far. Only a few have discussed the effects of globalization on the "Third World within," i.e. on local communities of colour. I think a serious spelling-out of the local impacts of global capitalism would be crucial to building a broader, more relevant and more powerful movement.

What I've learned from watching and working with community organizers around me is that building resistance and politicizing our communities takes years of thankless grunt work. I fear the anti-globalization hype has unintentionally produced "glory" activism (I've felt it)—the romance of being on the frontlines, taking up "arms," facing the repressive state reaction and all the attention afterwards. As anti-racist, anarchist writer Chris Crass points out in his essay "Looking to the Light of Freedom,"[6] this glorified activism makes it easy to forget the years of work, often hidden and often done by women, that have gone into shaping key social movements.

As Free Radical's L.A. Kauffman writes:

> Radicals whose activism largely consists of mobilizing for one big action after another … tend to develop very different politics from those who are deeply enmeshed in local organizing. There's a kind of rigor to nuts-and-bolts campaigning with concrete, immediate stakes—say, fighting to stop a power plant from being built in a low-income neighborhood with epidemic asthma rates—that privileges strategy over gestures. Without that grounding, it's all too easy to make the great militant error of elevating tactics to principles, rather than seeing them as tools, and to engage in confrontation for its own sake.[7]

I would start by asking where are the roots of the globalization problem. How can we aim for those roots in the long-term while addressing urgent needs for better living conditions? Who needs support, and how can we best give it without taking over? What creative, effective and accessible actions can we take while building radically alternative ways of relating to each other? What will it mean when these actions are "successful?"

To get more concrete, here's some sharp comments and suggestions from various organizers of the upcoming North American (NA) conference of Peoples' Global Action (PGA), a radical, grassroots network based in the 2/3 world, the Global South. One of PGA's hallmarks is a "rejection of all forms of oppression and exploitation such as patriarchy, white supremacy and imperialism."

Lesley Wood, a PGA organizer, writes, "Dynamics around networks are often dependent on who is at the table when the meeting starts. And I fear that not everyone will be there." She has suggested downscaling event costs to make them more accessible and asking more privileged groups to send someone from a movement that would otherwise not be represented.

Emphasizing the years it takes to build strong, diverse community alliances, another PGA organizer pointed out,

> To do alliance building does not mean that we just try to get indigenous groups or people of colour to attend a PGA conference, it means that a relationship of trust has been formed due to doing work that supports these organizations ... we need to be open to new ways of organizing.

NYC's Jane G. has suggested discussing "diversity of tactics" in "a room full of immigrant workers and people of colour," delaying the immediate launch of Peoples' Global Action-North America (PGA-NA) and prioritizing local tours by PGA reps from the Global South: "The visiting folks could talk up PGA directly with local groups here, and establish direct links of communication, thus allowing PGA-NA to build itself up without control or ownership (albeit unintentional) by the white middle-class anti-globalization crowd."

Many other activists, such as Ottawa activist Chelby Daigle, are committed to strengthening and resourcing the "parallel movement" of grassroots groups in communities of colour (of course, we stay aware that not all groups in these communities are grassroots) without waiting for the more mainstream anti-globalization organizations to wake up to these needs. A People of Colour Caucus in the "anti-globalization movement" in San Francisco has also focused on supporting people of colour in predominantly white organizations, a need with which some of us in Montréal can identify as well.

These are just a few ideas to get us started in our plan to ensure that the fight against imperialist, neo-liberal globalization is much more than a passing fad ready to be co-opted by unrepresentative organizations, politicians and even clever corporations. By seriously and systematically addressing racism and other oppressions in our own organizations, strategies and activities, I hope we can build a sustained, inclusive movement in which power and leadership (which exist even if we pretend to avoid it) can be transferred to all people.

Notes

1. See for example, Elizabeth "Betita" Martinez, "Where Was the Colour in Seattle? Looking for Reasons Why the Great Battle Was So White," Spring 2000, *www.tao.ca/~colours*
2. Helen Luu, Editorial, Colours of Resistance 'zine, *www.tao.ca/~colours*
3. Chris Dixon, "Finding Hope After Seattle: Rethinking Radical Activism and Building a Movement," *www.tao.ca/~colours*
4. Jane Gusbin, correspondence.
5. E-mail call-out by the organizers of this dialogue.
6. Chris Crass, 2000, "Looking to then Light of Freedom: Lessons from the Civil Rights Movement and Thoughts on Anarchist Orgaizing," *www.tao.ca/~colours*
7. *www.free-radical.org.*

Union march, Saturday, April 21. (Photo: Jo-Anne McArthur)

(Photo: Brandon Constant)

Building Sustainable Communities of Resistance

Sarah Lamble

Like many people who went to Québec City to protest the Summit of the Americas, I returned home with mixed feelings. On the one hand, I experienced what I find so inspiring about mass demonstrations: the intense energy of the crowd; the creativity of theatre activists and puppet performers; the passionate sharing of ideas among strangers; the incredible feeling of hope that overcomes me when surrounded by thousands of people who are struggling together for social change.

More importantly, I felt a sense of community—a place where people mattered. Preparing hot meals with the People's Potato and the Winnipeg Free Food Collective to feed hungry protesters, I knew that people's basic rights were important. Sharing space at the University of Laval where hundreds of strangers slept side-by-side for the night, I sensed the common decency and respect for one another. Marching through the streets as people waved and cheered from windows of office buildings, schools and houses, I experienced the power of solidarity. I also felt the spirit of community as people danced to music and celebrated anti-capitalist festivities at l'Ilôt Fleuri, and I saw the kindness and generosity of people from local neighbourhoods in Québec who opened their homes to protesters. These moments were proof of a community based on "human need, not corporate greed." These were moments when I felt like I was living in the kind of community that will create a different world.

On the other hand, this same community was the source of much frustration and disappointment, as it became obvious that it lacked a certain inclusiveness. First, the community was not a safe space for many people. Although I generally felt comfortable participating in the actions at Québec, I know many people did not feel the same sense of ease or entitlement to be part of the so-called "activist community." Others simply did not have access to the resources necessary for participation. Looking around at those who surrounded me on the streets, and particularly the people who came on buses from my community, I was struck by the overwhelmingly white middle-class composition of the crowd. Although the Indigenous Peoples Forum at the Peoples' Summit was attended by three hundred people, the Ontario Coalition Against Poverty was active in border and street actions, and over five hundred people from South and Central America joined North Americans in Québec, the general turnout was relatively privileged in terms of race and class.

Considering that the devastating impacts of the FTAA will be most felt by indigenous communities, women, people of low income, people of colour and those with special needs, the fact that such communities did not have a stronger presence in Québec indicates a problem. Whether it was the process of organizing, the lack of attention to economic or structural barriers, the forms of communication or perhaps the very protest actions themselves, something was clearly not working in our approach to openness to diversity.

Similarly, I was angered by the expressions of misogyny and homophobia that surfaced in protest signs, body language and strategy discussions. On the Friday march from Laval, I saw a protester use a gigantic cardboard penis painted like the U.S. flag to penetrate an anally-depicted image of the earth, a display which not only reiterated the norms of phallocentric power but also played upon homophobic discourses that liken the practice of anal sex to exploitation. Many people pointed and laughed at this display, as though it was merely a clever joke rather than a symptom of oppressive thinking. At the Saturday march, one union member carried a sign that equated feminism with dictatorship.

Gender inequality also was reinforced by the distribution of organizational work along traditional gender lines. I noticed, for example, that as groups were packing up to leave Laval on Sunday morning, it was primarily women who took the time to clean up garbage from the area. Likewise, most of the volunteers helping in the kitchen at l'Ilôt Fleuri were women, about 90 percent estimated one volunteer. It was generally agreed by those involved that when men did volunteer in the kitchen, they did one-time jobs, like washing a pot or carrying water, while women took on ongoing tasks which would last for hours.

Such patterns received scant attention in discussion; issues of gender and sexuality, like those of race and class, were often treated as peripheral concerns to questions of strategy. A friend told me of her decision not to distribute a zine she had created about women in the "anti-globalization movement," feeling that people weren't really interested and that it would probably end up as litter on the streets. Another friend declared that she felt more angered by the sexist and racist behaviour of protesters than by the behaviour of cops and that she almost returned home early because she couldn't handle such an oppressive environment.

Finally, hierarchies in the valuation of different forms of participation dismayed me. As attention in Québec became increasingly preoccupied with police confrontations at the fenced perimeter, other forms of participation—organizing buses, answering phones, doing legal work, providing food and childcare—were relegated to "support" roles. Sucking back tear gas seemed to be the primary criterion for a legitimate day of protest. Also seemingly forgotten were the local actions that took place in communities across Canada and the Americas.

Despite the tendency to blame the mainstream media for this focus, the CBC and the *Globe and Mail* were not the only culprits. Many activist websites posting stories and photos of the protest actions also became obsessed with street confrontations; it is still difficult to find online information about the Peoples' Summit; photos of local community initiatives are practically non-existent; and stories of behind-the-scenes work are relatively rare.

A friend told me that two women in his affinity group who had spent their time in the green zones felt marginalized because of their decision to stay away from high-risk arrest situations. On the bus ride home, they said that people wanted to discuss only what happened at the fence; other experiences were treated with disinterest and silence. These sentiments were confirmed in many conversations that took place at the various debriefing sessions I attended.

One woman said flatly, "There was no place for me at Québec."

All of these problems stem from a larger issue; the present conception of protest is lacking a broad inclusiveness. While the communities gathered in Québec were a welcoming place for many who attended, the absence and discomfort of others indicate limitations in openness and diversity. Consequently, the needs of some people were met while the needs of others were neglected. Moreover, many of the same forms of domination and oppression that protesters challenge in the exercise of global capitalist powers were reinscribed within our own communities. This is a serious issue, and one that I see reluctance to address.

Particularly when protesters continually get a bad rap from the corporate media and when there are so many existing divisions within communities around issues of analysis, tactics and violence, there is much at stake in opening up such a critique. But unless these issues are seriously addressed, the present movements and communities of dissent will be able neither to sustain themselves nor collectively overcome the forms of domination that they oppose in capitalist globalization.

Accordingly, the issue of inclusiveness should not be treated as an isolated problem; inclusiveness is directly related to the capacity to strengthen and expand communities of resistance in order to sustain them in the future. This is a problem that will not be solved by simply trying to recruit more people of colour, by asking more women to speak up or by providing more funding to people of low income. We need to start asking *why* our communities are not a safe space for everyone, what barriers people face in participation, why forms of oppression and domination persist within protest actions and what can be done about them.

These are difficult questions, but I see them as crucial to the viability of a long-term struggle against capitalist globalization. It is not tear gas, pepper spray and bullets that pose the greatest threat to the current "anti-globalization movements"; the greatest challenge is actually to put into practice, within our own communities, values that refuse all forms of domination and oppression.

These issues are not only relevant to the protests at Québec City; I have experienced these problems to one degree or another at every large demonstration that I have attended. While there have been many attempts to compare (and frequently romanticize) the 1999 protests at Seattle, I would argue that the same problems that existed in Québec existed there. They are symptomatic of larger problems within "anti-globalization movements" as a whole, problems in the way social activism is constructed and valued in the daily practices of our communities.

In response to these problems, a strategy of resistance must include a re-evaluation of the way in which we think about protest: first, by reworking the definitions of legitimate political action with long-term sustainability and inclusiveness in mind; and second, by replacing the use of reformist strategies regarding race, class, gender and sexuality with more radical approaches. Increasing inclusiveness is not a matter of inviting marginalized people into the organizational process; the process itself needs to change.

Reopening the definition of legitimate forms of protest against corporate globalization involves an interrogation of the meanings associated with the very terms used to describe actions and people. Part of my discomfort in using the term "anti-globalization movement" is, first, that it implies a single homogenous movement and, second, that it frequently refers to a series of mass demonstrations that supposedly began in Seattle and have continued in Washington, Melbourne, Prague, Québec and other parts of the world.

Such a definition not only frequently excludes the demonstrations that happen in Latin America, Africa and Asia—such as the mass protests against water privatization in Bolivia, the Narmada Valley Dam protests in India and the anti-IMF protests in Zimbabwe—it also excludes the less high-profile, everyday struggles that take place at the local community level across the globe. Such forms of resistance occur in public park spaces where homeless people lay out their sleeping mats for the night; in communities where indigenous peoples struggle to protect their lands and their culture; in women's shelters where volunteers organize against male violence; in classrooms where teachers fight against cutbacks; in rural communities where small farmers resist structural adjustment programs; and in sweatshops where workers struggle to form unions. These all are forms of resistance against the exploitation of the global free market and they must be recognized as such with inclusion, cooperation and solidarity.

Part of this redefinition of "anti-globalization" action must also include a resistance to "protest heroics"—the tendency to glorify the particular actions of individuals (often those actions to which people of privilege have access) and to neglect community struggles. I feel this tendency towards heroism every time I talk about "anti-globalization" actions and am asked, "Were you in Seattle? What about Washington? Did you get arrested? Tear gassed? Pepper sprayed?" People don't ask about what kinds of actions my community has organized. They want to know how many protests that I, the individual, have attended and what I did to cause trouble. I begin to feel as if every protest is a notch in my activist belt and I'm getting silver studs every time I've been doused with chemicals.

But who gets to have these credentials as an activist? A pregnant woman, for example, is not in a position to expose herself to chemical weapons. Likewise, an international student may not be able to risk losing her university degree by facing deportation should she be arrested. Others, particularly people of colour who face greater police harassment and brutality, may even risk death by participating in these types of actions. The 1995 murder of Dudley George at Ipperwash Provincial Park by the Ontario Provincial Police is a chilling reminder of the risks Aboriginal people face when participating in peaceful protest. The legacy of police threats continued at Québec City: Aboriginal protest organizers were harassed by police and a meeting planned for a Huron community outside Québec City was cancelled after intimidating visits by the RCMP.

In choosing the kind of action in which they will participate, people encounter significant barriers, barriers that explain why protest crowds are so often comprised of people of privilege. Efforts must be made to break down those barriers so that the diversity of people who wish to participate can choose to do so, and the spectrum of legitimate political action must also be broadened and respected.

My intention here is not to undermine the courage of those who put their bodies on the line in street protests, those who expose themselves to chemical warfare, confront police brutality, spend time in jail and face the repercussions of criminal charges. I have been in that position, and I know that it is not an easy place to be. Nor am I taking a stance against confrontational street tactics, which I believe to be an important form of protest.

One of my frustrations in Québec—one that I also experienced at the IMF–World Bank protest in Washington and the OAS protest in Windsor—was that organized labour, NGO groups and other sectors of "civil society" did not take a more aggressive approach on the street. Had the fifty thousand people in the legal march joined the protesters at the fence, there might have been a much different outcome in Québec. If there had been a collective decision to march through the fence, even six thousand cops with tear gas and pepper spray would have been no match for such massive numbers. Had such an action been strategically organized, people could have mobilized to ensure maximum safety for those at high risk of police brutality and chemical exposure.

Even still, the symbolism of dismantling parts of the fence was a tremendous victory at Québec, and I do not wish to detract from that accomplishment. I also do not wish to demonize those who choose what is often described by the press as "violent" tactics. I am aware that many people, particularly those who live on the streets and are routinely harassed and beaten by cops, often do not have access to other resources for protest. These days, political leaders pay little attention to conventional forms of protest; petitions, letter-writing campaigns and rallies are frequently ignored by those in power. Street aggression—whether it be smashing bank windows or retaliating against police violence—in its physical and economic threat to the corporate and state elite has become an important tool of survival for many.

Therefore what I am questioning here is not the use of such tactics but the amount of attention given to these actions in proportion to other forms of protest. These street tactics are *one part* of the larger struggle, and they mean very little without the organizational work, planning and everyday strengthening of the communities behind them.

Long-term struggles also require a rethinking of how positions of privilege are maintained within activist communities and why exclusionary practices happen in the first place. Too often reformist strategies are used to approach issues of race, class, gender, sexuality and ability. This logic assumes that the existing system of organization is working; it doesn't need to change, it simply requires wider participation from more diverse communities. In such strategies, efforts are made to include marginalized people in organizational processes, but the processes themselves don't change. As a result, the causes of marginalization are ignored and structural forms of domination are relegated to the periphery of the discussion. Race, gender and class become add-ons to the "main" discussion.

For example, I have attended numerous teach-ins where a gender-parity speakers list is established (the speakers alternate between men and women to allow for equal speaking opportunities). Despite these efforts for speaker equity, there are consistently two or three times as many men than women at the microphone, and few people ever openly ask why this is happening. While equity speakers lists are important, they need to be complemented by efforts to address the root causes of gender imbalances.

Similarly, attempts often are made at panel discussions to ensure that there is representation from women and people of colour, but panel topics and debate questions frequently fail to put issues of race, gender and class at the centre of discussion. As a result, it is consistently women who must bring up gender issues, people of colour who must bring up questions of racism and people of low income who must bring up issues of class.

A further problem involves access to forms of communication. E-mail has been one of the major forms of communication in organizing "anti-globalization" actions, but more than half of Canadians, particularly those of low income, the elderly and those who have disabilities, do not have access to the internet. One can send out thousands of e-mails about poverty-related actions, but if homeless people cannot get access to the e-mails, their participation in those actions will be limited.

Without asking who is being excluded in activist communities and why, efforts to remedy the problem are reduced to minority recruitment campaigns. And who wants to take part in something that is dominated by someone else's agenda? Movements towards real inclusiveness must include a willingness to interrogate positions of privilege and transform existing structures and practices of exclusion.

The issues raised here are not simple problems, and they will not be resolved overnight. To question fundamental assumptions and challenge foundational goals is to participate in a long-term struggle towards meaningful change, an effort that takes time, energy and commitment. Building nonoppressive communities requires hard work, dedication and determination, but these are efforts that we cannot do without. The capacity to build long-term and globally connected communities of resistance is dependent on sustainability, diversity and inclusiveness. The space for these values exists within present and future communities. As has been shown by the spirit of hope and courage expressed by those who gathered in Québec and those who are organizing against capitalist globalization in communities across the planet, there currently exists enormous potential for revolutionary change. A different world is indeed possible. It is a question of whether we are willing to take up that challenge.

(Photo: Jo-Anne McArthur)

Epilogue

Editorial Collective

Without a doubt, the events in Québec City politicized, even radicalized, many people across Canada and the U.S. The struggle against the FTAA in particular and corporate globalization in general has found renewed vigour due to the intensity of the actions on the part of both protesters and police. This event will go down in Canadian his/herstory, along with recent police state responses at Oka/Kanesatake in 1991, Gustafsen Lake in 1995, Ipperwash in 1995, the APEC Summit of 1997 and the OAS meeting of 2000, as prime examples of the true democratic nature of the Canadian state. The much-discussed "criminalization of dissent" has finally made its way to the mainstream, and many people don't like what they see.

The gathering in Québec was inspiring and much more than a symbolic statement, as extensive organizational work went into mobilizing such a large amount of people. The Québec City-based organizations did great outreach work and were ever-helpful to visiting groups. Before thousands of people converged on the city, one local organizer had this metaphor for the existing organizational barriers in Québec:

> Well, to begin with, there aren't that many activists in Québec and not much infrastructure to hold such a big event. It's kind of like if suddenly, the people who run the local hockey rink had to put on the Olympics, had to house thousands of people, feed people, do all the local groundwork. It hasn't been easy, but we think it'll work out.

We would like to thank all the *militants/tes* for their great work. *Milles mercis!*

We would also like to underline their attempts not only at mobilizing people for the big event but also at raising awareness in their local communities about the FTAA. Months before the summit, workshops were held in Québec and Montréal on an almost weekly basis. All of this work showed up continuously in Québec, whether it was those people who gladly refilled water bottles with their hoses in the St-Jean Baptiste neighbourhood; those hundreds who, after going to workshops, decided on "adopting a protester"; those thousands of local residents who took part in the huge march on Saturday; those who set up makeshift medic centres on their porches or even in their apartments; or those who simply smiled and showed their support by saying "thank you." The efforts of local organizers were omnipresent.

Of course, the same is true for countless local community groups and individuals across the Americas. Over a hundred thousand people took to their streets during the weekend of the summit. Solidarity actions tend to be forgotten in the attention given to mass actions such as those in Québec. We readily admit to being disappointed at not being able to move away from a nearly Québec-only focus for this project and hope that similar projects will be more community focused in the future.

In Latin America, there were events in countless locales: the Canadian embassy in Quito, Ecuador, was occupied by a loose coalition of students and workers; nearly one hundred arrests were made at a large solidarity march in Sao Paulo, Brazil; just two weeks before the summit thousands of people took to the streets of Buenos Aires, Argentina, to protest a trade ministers' meeting there, and many of the same people took to the streets again during the summit. And, similar to events on the Canada–U.S. border, nearly one hundred buses from Brazil were denied entry into Argentina during the trade ministers' mini-summit.

Likewise, there were nearly a dozen actions on North American borders during the weekend. The protesters' message was clear: "Free movement to people, not 'free' trade!" On the U.S.–Mexico border at Tijuana–San Diego, there was a five-thousand-strong march, followed by presentations by local community members from both sides of the international border. At Blaine, Washington, a similar march took nearly seven thousand people over into the U.S. to protest the FTAA. Actions in Buffalo, New York; Burlington, Vermont; Windsor/ Detroit; Jackman, Maine; and, of course, at Akwesasne in Mohawk Territory all underlined the incredible importance of mobilizing at a community level. The Ontario Coalition Against Poverty (OCAP) and Akwesasne efforts give us great hope that future planning for mass actions will make the necessary links between globalization and community struggles.

For example, often when there is talk of the detrimental effects of trade agreements like the FTAA, the experiences of Majority World countries tend to be separated from those of North American communities. Little attention goes towards making links and looking at how our own communities are affected by the same neo-liberal agenda. It's important to recognize that North America's increasing gap between rich and poor; its ethics and practices around domestic workers; its current racist, sexist and classist immigration/refugee laws; its rise of homelessness and sweat shops in urban and sometimes rural centres; its feminization of poverty; and its near privatization of health care and education are all intertwined with similar struggles across the globe.

Thus it's crucial to keep in mind, especially as privileged North Americans, that the struggle against globalization, capitalism and the possible effects of the FTAA did not start in Québec, nor did it start in Seattle in 1999. Although these big protests were a symbol of the growing concern among mostly privileged citizens over the erosion of their rights, there are countless communities, individuals and organizations continuously doing the behind-the-scenes community-based work who are too often excluded when any talk of the so-called "anti-globalization movement" arises. But due to their continued lack of basic human rights, their long history of organized resistance and their everyday experiences, they are well-versed in both the damaging effects of globalization in their own communities and the less than "democratic" way in which the same detrimental, neo-liberal policies currently fuelling globalization are being implemented at home. However, they are seldom acknowledged as "experts" and are rarely given an opportunity to share their divergent experiences with the broader community of mostly privileged "activists." We can begin to see change but making these all-important community links cannot wait any longer.

Having said this, the anti-capitalist/globalization movement is growing. It's not growing as one central umbrella organization; it's growing as individuals continue to educate and organize themselves at a community level. Those who were able to make it to Québec City and other mass actions are only one part of the broader, worldwide coalition to counter the often unseen and unheard of effects of U.S.-style imperialism and neocolonialism, which are often masked by terminology such as "development" and "globalization." For there to be any movement forward, we must acknowledge and support grassroots initiatives. Again, for the mass protest tactic to be most effective, it must carry on community struggles.

Of course, the question of tactics is always omnipresent. During the production of this book, we received numerous accounts from people criticizing the lack of numbers at the frontlines near the fence. While it's agreed that the fence was an insult to any notion of democracy and consequently demanded attention, there seemed to be much romaticization of frontline action. Some may have perceived frontliners as being "hard-core" activists. The true reality tells us that it is equally demanding to incorporate the struggle into one's everyday life. We aren't trying to criticize those at the frontlines, but we need to take a deeper look at the glorification that we give those frontline actions.

However, many who were involved in the more confrontational actions were local Québécois of the working-class neighbourhoods around the perimeter. Many were also street youth, whose only means of expressing rage and dissatisfaction is through direct action. This reality needs to be discussed. We need to shift our focus from the "violence/nonviolence" debate to the conditions that allow for little option other than the use of force against an otherwise violent system. What is truly violent is the violence of poverty, the violence of oppressions, of sexism, racism, classism, homophobia, ableism, etc.

The constant use of war-like terminology by protesters in Québec is suggestive of the life experiences of many who attended the actions. While the brutality of the police-state's actions cannot be denied, it would be misleading not to mention the violence and extremity of war experienced daily by others in our world. There are many here in Canada who face police brutality on a regular basis: street youth, people of low or no income, single mothers, First Nations people, people of colour, street workers, psychiatric survivors, people with mental health problems, immigrants and refugees, lesbians/gays/bis, transsexuals and transgendered people, etc. Many, if not most, of those who were present in Québec City have the privilege of not having to experience and/or acknowledge the unjust practices undertaken by the elite of this hemisphere.

Instead of stopping short and focusing our attention and outrage on arbitrary arrests and degrading treatment in prisons, beatings and tear gas in Québec City, we need to support the work of communities and local organizations already involved in such struggles against the state and the police.

On a final note, as evidenced in Québec City, there exists much potential for the creation of alternate systems and safe community spaces in the future. What is obvious, however, is that this work must be incorporated into local decision-making processes and organizational work. Nonhierarchical and anti-oppressive, –classist, –sexist, –racist, –heterosexist, –ableist) spaces are a necessary starting point in the struggle for a more equitable and just society.

(Photo: Richard Swift)

(Photo:Scott Harris)

References

Websites of Relevance to the FTAA, Quebec City Protests and Globalization

http://www.sommetdespeuples.org/en/ — Second Peoples' Summit of the Americas

http://www.web.net/comfront/quebec.htm — Second Peoples' Summit of the Americas

http://www.tao.ca/~ocap/ — Ontario Coalition Against Poverty

http://www.tao.ca/~kev/belly/en/ftaaag.html — FTAA, Food and Agriculture

http://www.tao.ca/~colours/ — Colours of Resistance

http://nanaimo.ark.com/~amanra/quebec.html — a20 (Quebec City, April 2001)

http://www.web.net/comfront/ — Common Frontiers Home Page

http://www.stopftaa.org/ — Stop the FTAA

http://www.web.ca/~comfront/alts4americas/eng/eng.html — Alternatives for the Americas Building a Peoples' Hemispheric Agreement

http://www.sommetdespeuples.org/en/qui/index.html — Second Peoples' Summit of the Americas

http://quebec.indymedia.org/ — Centre for Media Alternatives of Quebec 2001

http://www.geocities.com/ftaadiary/ — An FTAA Diary

http://www.straightgoods.com/FTAA/ — Straight Goods' Quebec Summit Home Page

http://www.canadians.org/campaigns/campaigns-tradepub-ftaa2.html — Council of Canadians: Campaigns: Trade and Investment

Websites of Some FTAA Protest Organizers

http://www.tao.ca/~clac/ — The Anti-Capitalist Convergence

http://www.quebec2001.net/ — The Anti-Capitalist Convergence

http://www.oqp2001.org/ — Opération Québec Printemps 2001 (French)

http://www.alternatives.ca/salami/ — Operation SalAMI

http://www.multimania.com/gomm/ — Le Groupe Opposé à la Mondialisation des Marchés... à Montréal. (French)

http://www.quebeclegal.org/ — Quebec Legal Collective

Some Sites with Links

http://www.indymedia.org/ — Independent Media Center

http://www.ocsj.ca/ — The Ontario Coalition for Social Justice

www.maquilasolidarity.org — Maquila Solidarity Network

www.canadians.org — Council of Canadians

http://www.corporatewatch.org.uk/ — Corporate Watch

www.mob4glob.ca/ — The Toronto Mobilization for Global Justice

http://www.policyalternatives.ca/ — Canadian Centre for Policy Alternatives

http://www.rabble.ca/ — rabble.ca